Agility

Agility

Management Principles for a Volatile World

Michael Edmondson, PhD

BEP

BUSINESS EXPERT PRESS

Leader in applied, concise business books

First published in 2021 by
Business Expert Press, LLC
222 East 46th Street, New York, NY 10017
www.businessexpertpress.com

ISBN-13: 978-1-95334-944-6 (paperback)
ISBN-13: 978-1-95334-945-3 (e-book)

Business Expert Press Human Resource Management and Organizational Behavior Collection

Collection ISSN: 1946-5637 (print)
Collection ISSN: 1946-5645 (electronic)

First edition: 2021

10 9 8 7 6 5 4 3 2 1

Printed in the United States of America.

To Amanda, Kiersten, and Jonathan

Description

Agility: Management Principles for a Volatile World fills a tremendous need in the marketplace for a practical set of principles to help managers become more agile. Today's volatile, uncertain, complex, and ambiguous (VUCA) world has created a dynamic, ever-changing, and hypercompetitive global marketplace, challenging managers to think differently. The apprehension of the present moment experienced by managers across industries, sectors, and markets demands a new way of understanding the nuances involved with navigating today's chaos to achieve and sustain growth. With the speed of change, disruption, and transformation expected to increase exponentially now is the opportune time for organizations to rethink the common management paradigms of power (we are bigger), speed (we move faster), or force (we can acquire). Agility, more so, than power, speed, or force is the *Kairos* for managers today. In archery, *Kairos,* the ancient Greek word for a proper or opportune time for action, denotes the moment in which an arrow may be fired with sufficient force to reach a target. Now is an opportune time for managers to become more agile and shift their position from one of planning, organizing, staffing, directing, or controlling to one of being a curator, architect, conductor, humanist, advocate, and pioneer. This shift from doing to being is paramount for the agile manager. *Agility: Management Principles for a Volatile World* provides readers with a list of principles associated with each role of the modern agile manager and is required reading for individuals from small to medium-sized businesses, large corporations, nonprofit organizations, and government offices.

Keywords

business; leadership; management; agility; global business

Contents

Other Books by Edmondson

The Relevance of the Humanities to the 21st Century Workplace
Strategic Thinking and Writing
Success: Theory and Practice
Major in Happiness: Debunking the College Major Fallacies
Marketing Your Value: 9 Steps to Navigate Your Career

What People Are Saying

Dr. Edmonson's sixth book Agility: Management Principles for a Volatile World is a thought-provoking journey through the Six Functions of the Agile Manager. Each function provides a roadmap for managers on how to navigate in today's unpredictable and highly volatile environment. In retrospect, this book should be a requirement for all managers especially those starting out on their managerial journey. **—John Donnellan, DPS, MBA, Chair Management Department New Jersey City University School of Business**

If you're waiting for things to "get back to normal" then this book probably isn't the book for you. But, if you're hoping to learn how to adapt your management style for the current reality where the "new normal" is ever-changing, then you might be ready for this book. If you are ready to question "every aspect of the approach, methodology, biases, and deeply held assumptions," that you have about how to be a successful leader in the volatile world that we find ourselves, then you'll want to read Agility: Management Principles for a Volatile World. **—Jason D. Finley, Career Development Coordinator. Adult Education Coordinator, Randolph Technical Career Center**

Today's leaders—more than ever—must respond to ever shifting realities within their organizations. Our social and economic realities require leaders to move nimbly among people and processes in a way that provides direction and focus, but also responsiveness. Edmondson's work outlines the attributes that truly agile leaders should embody to bring about real and sustainable growth. He guides leaders to fully own their roles as curator, architect, conductor, humanist, advocate, and architect to create spaces that not only grow, but evolve as true learning organizations. **—Allison Rodman, Founder, The Learning Loop, Leadership Coach**

In Major in Happiness: Debunking the College Major Fallacies, Edmondson clearly debunks the myth that only certain college majors achieve greater success than others. More importantly, he maps a process to achieve and retain success and happiness which are two sides of a coin. A must read for parents and students thinking of going to college. —**Arun Tilak, Director, Center for Emerging Technology & Entrepreneurial Studies, Cameron University**

In Major in Happiness: Debunking the College Major Fallacies, Edmondson's theories are accompanied by practical exercises that will be of value to students and their parents as they navigate a pathway through the complex interactions of study and work. He also points to two critical skills: teamwork and listening skills we expect and rarely teach. This book adds significantly to the debate about education and is a must read for incoming and exiting graduates and their parents. —**John Christian, President/CEO, CAPA, The Global Education Network**

Major in Happiness: Debunking the College Major Fallacies is truly a thought-provoking book. This book certainly puts majors in perspective and the importance of doing what you love. This is a must read for parents of college bound students. —**Cindy Szadokierski, Executive Director, The Edge Program, Randolph-Macon College**

Using strong research blended with a practical, clear writing style, Dr. Edmondson provides perspective and advice that the current generation of students (and parents) desperately needs to hear. So many young people quickly abandon their passions and dreams to pursue majors and careers that they believe are 'necessary' to achieve success and satisfaction in their vocational and personal lives. Edmondson pulls back the curtain on the misconceptions and fallacies that fuel that thinking and outlines a compelling argument for the pursuit of a life driven by calling, purpose, and passion. As a professor in one of the disciplines that is often marginalized, I frequently work with students who are wrestling with the exact tensions that Edmondson describes, and I will certainly recommend Major in Happiness: Debunking the College Major Fallacies as a resource for those students in the future. —**Jeremy Osborn, PhD, Associate Professor of Communication, Cornerstone University**

Major in Happiness: Debunking the College Major Fallacies presents an eye-opening presentation of the unique challenges of the 21st century college student. Edmondson offers more than just data to support his beliefs that perseverance, adaptability and life-long learning are keys to success. He provides an array of self-assessment tools to help students—and professionals alike—evaluate their unique value to corporations and the world. As a professor, this book has changed the way I will mentor my students. A must-read for all of us navigating through this quickly-changing landscape and trying to find our place in it. —**Laura Grayson Roselli, Professor, Rowan College at Burlington County, and Biopharmaceutical Consultant, Kinetic Knowledge, LLC**

Dr. Edmondson provides graduates and professionals with a road map to bring to practice Jonathan Winters' quote, 'If your ship doesn't come in, swim out to meet it.' Not only does he make a compelling case for swimming to meet the ship, he also provides readers with the knowledge of how to swim, and to swim in the right direction: the 'Assess, Brand, and Communicate' approach. Marketing Your Value: 9 Steps to Navigate Your Career is an excellent read for college students, recent graduates and mid-career professionals as they navigate their careers and prepare for the next step towards their professional goals. —**Pareena Lawrence, PhD, Provost and Dean of the College, Professor of Economics, Augustana College, Rock Island, Illinois**

Michael Edmondson brings many years of advising emerging undergraduates on the challenges and practical strategies for launching and adapting a career in a rapidly changing global economy. While giving substantial attention to self-marketing in a digital age, Edmondson's approach is founded self-evaluation—very much in the liberal-arts tradition—asking readers to assess their values and abilities in relation to opportunities and to regard the job search as a flexible, ever-changing process of self-exploration and assessment more than orientation to a fixed goal. In the tradition of What Color Is Your Parachute and What Should I Do With My Life?, Marketing Your Value: 9 Steps to Navigate Your Career is likely to be invaluable to anyone who is entering the job market, considering a change of direction, or advising those who are. —**William Pannapacker, PhD, Professor of English, Director of the Andrew W. Mellon Foundation Scholars Program in the Arts and Humanities, Faculty Director of the Great Lakes Colleges Association's Digital Liberal Arts Initiative, Hope College**

In Marketing Your Value: 9 Steps to Navigate Your Career, Michael asks the tough and provoking questions that many of us struggle with on a day-to-day basis, such as understanding our personal mission, unveiling our distractions, and coming to terms with the major influence we have in our career development. This book provides an opportunity for professionals from any age, background, and industry the time to understand themselves through a series of thoughtful and challenging reflections and activities. By doing this, Michael guides us back to our core to help us rediscover our values and use this knowledge as the foundation to successfully navigate a meaningful, and purposeful career. —**Yalitza M. Negron, M.S. Ed., Associate Director, Office of Academic Community Engagement, Siena College**

Marketing Your Value: 9 Steps to Navigate Your Career is an outstanding read and is applicable to any working individual's life. Dr. Edmondson's writing is clear, concise, and informative, a true reflection of the hardships many professionals, both young and old, face in today's highly competitive workforce. Through its various exercises and practices, Marketing Your Value will help anyone understand the tools, habits, and behaviors that are necessary when traveling the road to success. Dr. Edmondson has played an integral role in the launch of my career and continues to provide me with valuable insight along my professional journey. His immense knowledge on the topics of marketing and branding clearly shines through in this publication. —**Emily Nemeth, Admissions Manager of Ladywood High School, Livonia, MI**

Marketing Your Value is a practical resource filled with helpful tools and interesting anecdotes for assessing, branding, and communicating one's value—a valuable resource for anyone making a transition. I look forward to sharing it with my students. —**Steve VanderVeen, PhD, Director of the Center for Faithful Leadership at Hope College, Professor of Management**

Marketing Your Value: 9 Steps to Navigate Your Career is a practical book that illustrates how to successfully navigate career challenges in today's economy. —**Sheila Curran, President, Curran Consulting Group and author of Smart Moves for Liberal Arts Grads: Finding a Path to Your Perfect Career**

Michael Edmondson has written the handbook for those striving to succeed in the new millennium. Instead of a run-of-the-mill self-help book, Success Theory and Practice connects the science, philosophy, and habits that drive individuals to success in today's marketplace. Success isn't a secret, and this book offers a roadmap for anyone willing to take on the challenge. —**Adam Cirucci, Political Consultant and Journalist**

Michael connects the dots in his book Success: Theory and Practice where the rubber meets the road with his 7 Characteristics of Success. He demonstrates the practical traits, backed up by fascinating research, to help you unfold your own success story. —**John P. Clark, CFP®, Financial Advisor and Retirement Living Expert**

Michael Edmonson's Success: Theory and Practice is equal parts research and vision. This is how we do success in the 21st century: not only do we seek to improve our lot, but also our relationships, our self-awareness, and our world. Success is not either/or, but both/and. —**Evan Harris, Co-owner of Tapas Yoga Shala**

Michael Edmonson's newest book Success: Theory and Practice is an absolute must read for both anyone entering the job market and those looking for growth in both their professional and personal lives. This book is not your everyday book on success, as it touches on the success of many, but lets you in on the mental and emotional challenges each faced throughout the journey. As quoted in the book from George Bernard Shaw 'People are always blaming their circumstances for what they are. I do not believe in circumstances. The people who get on in this world are the people who get up and look for the circumstances that they want, and if they can't find them, make them.' This book makes you want to find the circumstances you want in life. —**Rocco Marrari, National Accounts Manager for EBE Technologies**

Success: Theory and Practice is a must read for anyone who is interested achieving personal and professional success. Personal and professional growth is a key to success in our careers in this ever changing environment. Dr. Edmondson provides questions to ask ourselves periodically as a performance temperature check along with some quizzes. He also provides real life examples of successful individuals and traits they implemented to achieve their success. —**Robert Sauselein, CHST, HazTek, Inc.**

Dr. Edmondson's writing style is clear and concise while including research relevant to theory and the practice of success. Choosing to read Success: Theory and Practice will challenge yourself to examine your own personal traits while receiving applicable advice on how to engage in successful behaviors, thus leading to personal and professional growth. —**Shelly Thomas Vroman, NP**

Strategic Thinking and Writing is a must read for students and business professionals looking to enhance their strategic thinking and writing skills. Throughout the book, Dr. Edmondson provides readers the opportunity to perform thinking exercises and self-awareness checks which I found to be that are extremely helpful. Dr. Edmondson reminds us that writing is a process that we need to respect in order to produce a high-quality product. —**Monique Oudijk, Bayada Home Health Care**

Thinking and writing well is one of the single most important traits you can have in the business world. Knowing how to think and write well helps you to perform and convey great ideas in your workplace. Dr. Edmondson's Strategic Thinking and Writing will help you capture your ideas and showcase them to your professional audience. Displaying great ideas with skill gives you power that is well deserved, and this book will help you achieve that easily. —**Katie Calabrese, National Association for Community College Entrepreneurship**

In an era when more time is spent on constant tweeting than on critical thinking, Michael Edmondson provides an important reminder that the path to success won't be found by staying glued to a device. Strategic Thinking and Writing is a guide for effectively using the one key element needed to gain the upper hand in any challenging situation: your own thought process. —**Ronald Panarotti, Rider University**

Dr. Edmondson's Strategic Thinking and Writing is a fascinating piece of literature that will help you remain focused, motivated, and engaged in the art of critical thinking. This book captures real life success stories and provides magnificent exercises, each designed to help people improve their strategic thinking and writing skills. This book has encouraged me to open up my mind, increase my self-awareness, and continuously strive for clear and efficient thinking. **—Martha Redondo, Princeton Theological Seminary**

Acknowledgments

My first management experience occurred during my undergraduate days at Cabrini College in Radnor, Pennsylvania. While working for the maintenance department to help pay my tuition, the college had a partnership with the nearby Don Guanella School that provided a quality of life, care, and service to persons with developmental disabilities based on the core values of compassion, charity, excellence, justice, and dignity. The organization was responsive to meeting the individual physical, emotional, spiritual, and social needs of the people we serve. Students from Don Guanella would be assigned to my shifts and throughout the four years it was an honor for me to work with those young men. It was here, during my formative years of leadership and management training, that the term service leadership, or servant, became familiar to me firsthand. Treating these young men with developmental disabilities taught me a great deal about myself, but also the world of leadership and management. As a leader my job was to model appropriate behavior and as a manager the task before me was to have each student help me complete the day's work assignments. Interactions from those days still resonate with me some three decades later. Little did it occur to me then, but those experiences would cement the foundation of a career built on service, agility, and compassion.

With a career spanning K to 12 education, teaching at the undergraduate and graduate level, serving as a consultant to small and medium-sized businesses as well as corporations and nonprofit organizations, and most recently as an executive at the university level, those three traits of service, agility, and compassion, born decades ago, have become a mainstay in a world that grows more volatile, uncertain, complex, and ambiguous with each passing day. Leadership and management are synonymous with how one treats others. It is, in short, that simple. Sadly, so few people understand how to treat others, and therefore, fail in their leadership and management responsibilities. Decades of witnessing, experiencing, and noticing countless examples of poor leadership and ineffective management have been the catalyst for writing *Agility: Management Principles for a Volatile World*. My hope is that, in some small way, the functions and principles outlined here can help managers at all levels learn about those three characteristics instilled in me decades ago: service, agility, and compassion.

My acknowledgments include a host of people who have supported me throughout the writing and publication process. At Business Expert Press, a continued debt of gratitude to the entire team, especially Rob Zwettler, Charlene Kronstedt, and Sheri Dean. This is my sixth publication with the Business Expert Press team and their efforts are greatly appreciated as they have provided tremendous support to help me publish six books in six years. Thank you for your time, effort, and encouragement along the way. My gratitude also goes out to John Donnellan, Jason D. Finley, and Allison Rodman for their review of the manuscript prior to publication. Dr. Donnellan was particularly helpful as he provided a good deal of time to discuss numerous topics covered in this book.

As always, a great deal of gratitude goes to my wife Lori for her constant support throughout the writing process. In her own way, she has taught me about service, agility, and compassion when it came to raising our two children, Amanda and Jonathan. Finally, this book is dedicated to Amanda, her wife Kiersten, and Jonathan as they have matured into young professionals embarking on their own leadership and management journeys. While they are each traveling down three different career paths, early indications of their leadership and management styles illustrate they are well on their way to demonstrating the highest levels of service, agility, and compassion.

Introduction

The Definition of Agility

Just how important is agility? According to Gallup's research published in 2019 "Organizations that aren't agile and that don't have the capacity to adapt quickly will be overcome by their competitors—or put out of business."[1] In its 2019 *Global CEO Outlook* titled *Agile or Irrelevant: Redefining Resilience*, the consulting firm KPMG concluded: "A successful CEO is an agile CEO. Over two-thirds of chief executive officers believe that agility is the new currency of business. If they fail to adapt to a constantly changing world, their business will become irrelevant."[2] Moreover, McKinsey's research details how "the agile organization is dawning as the new dominant organizational paradigm. Rather than organization as machine, the agile organization is a living organism."[3] Agility is here to stay as long as the global marketplace keeps disrupting the way people live, work, and do just about everything around the world. Moreover, the emergence of the COVID-19 global pandemic during the completion of this book stressed organizations around world and exposed significant issues, concerns, and problems. To address the pressure points made visible by the unexpected crisis, organizations looking to create a sustainable future had as their new priority "the making of meaningful investments

---

[1] Clifton, J., and J. Harter. 2019. "It's the Manager: From Gallup, Based on the Largest Global Study on the Future of Work." *SlideShare* presentation dated June 16, 2019. https://slideshare.net/ShivShivakumar1/book-summary-its-the-manager

[2] KPMG. *Agile or Irrelevant: Redefining Resilience, 2019 Global CEO Outlook.* https://drive.google.com/file/d/1Q3aNiey6XPAaNyc-CbFReBQ10uCqZWk6/view

[3] "The Five Trademarks of Agile Organizations." January 2018, *McKinsey Report.* https://mckinsey.com/business-functions/organization/our-insights/the-five-trademarks-of-agile-organizations

in human capital to build an agile, flexible workforce."[4] As such, it is important to begin with a definition.

There are as many definitions of agility as there are people defining the word. The standard definition comes from the *Merriam-Webster's Dictionary*, which defines agility as "being agile" and agile as "marked by ready ability to move with quick easy grace or having a quick resourceful and adaptable character." The etymology of agile originates from Latin *agilis* and from *agere* "do." As the world went from a connected to a hyperconnected global economy during the last 15 years, agility became a focus point for business writers since managers needed to determine how best to navigate the dynamics driving the disruptive marketplace and *do* something. In Google Book's N Gram Viewer analysis, *agile* was barely mentioned from 1800 to 1995. The period from 1995 to the present marked a significant increase in the use of the word agile and the future trend continues upward.[5]

In *Agility: How to Navigate the Unknown and Seize Opportunity in a World of Disruption* (2019), Leo M. Tilman and General Charles Jacoby (Ret.) focused on the organization and defined agility as "The organizational capacity to effectively detect, assess and respond to environmental changes in ways that are purposeful, decisive and grounded in the will to win." In *Emotional Agility: Get Unstuck, Embrace Change, and Thrive in Work and Life (2016)*, Susan David broadened the definition of agility to include emotions and wrote: "Emotional agility—being flexible with your thoughts and feelings so that you can respond optimally to everyday situations-is a key to well-being and success." In *The Agility Shift: Creating AGILE and Effective Leaders, Teams, and Organizations* (2015), Pamela Meyer focused on what she labeled the agility shift: "The Agility Shift is the intentional development of the competence, capacity, and confidence to learn, adapt, and innovation in changing contexts for sustainable success." In *Leadership Agility: Five Levels of Mastery for Anticipating and Initiating Change* (2006), Bill Joiner and Stephen Josephs define agility as "the ability to take wise and effective action amid complex, rapidly changing

---

[4] Tincher, S. 2020. "An Agile Workforce will be Key to Success Post-Pandemic." *Market Insights*, July 1, 2020. https://benefitspro.com/2020/07/01/an-agile-workforce-will-be-key-to-success-post-pandemic/?slreturn=20200602083402

[5] Google Books N Gram Viewer for agile available at https://tinyurl.com/ngramagile

conditions." They use the words leader and manager interchangeably and believe there are five levels to the agile leader: expert, achiever, catalyst, cocreator, and synergist and three functional areas of pivotal conversations, team leadership, and organizational leadership. Each examination into agility provides important points to consider in the ongoing dialogue. As organizations look to achieve and sustain growth in today's ever-changing landscape, the value of agility will only increase.

In this publication, agility refers *to the manager's ability to increase their self-awareness, think differently, and create the organizational change required to achieve and sustain growth.* This definition emphasizes self-awareness as the foundational requirement for any manager to achieve if they want their organization to become more agile. While the thousands of other books, articles, and resources on management provide wonderful learning opportunities, this book will go beyond the traditional approaches and challenge the manager in a volatile world to accomplish the following three tasks in order to increase their self-awareness.

- *Increase reflection time*: Instead of responding to emails, putting out the proverbial fires, and attending endless meetings, the agile manager needs more time alone to reflect upon the bigger questions, issues, and concerns facing the organization. The amount of reflection time is in direct proportion to the amount of responsibility. Therefore, the greater the level of responsibility, the more reflection time is needed.
- *Ask relevant questions*: During the increased reflection time, the agile manager operating in a volatile world needs to ask relevant questions. The questions need to focus on their internal awareness as well as their external presence within the organization. To assist the reader this publication provides over 100 questions to answer.
- *Challenge assumptions*: As the manager asks relevant questions, it is imperative they challenge previously held assumptions. There can be little progress toward agility at the organizational level if the manager is unable to demonstrate an agile mind. Employees, clients, and others would value the flexibility of thought, the elasticity of attitude, and the audacity of vision that accompany challenging one's assumptions.

Since professional development is linked directly to personal growth, engaging in each of these three activities on a regular basis will help increase one's self-awareness. Armed with a deeper sense of self, the manager can help the organization achieve the level of agility required to achieve and sustain growth in a volatile world.

While the literature on agility and business continues to grow, the amount of research on managers maintains a fast pace as well. During the last decade, dozens of books have joined the best-selling titles from generations past and emerged as important titles to read. Some of the more talked about publications dealing with some aspect of management include: Jim Clifton and Jim Harter, *It's the Manager: Gallup finds the quality of managers and team leaders is the single biggest factor in your organization's long-term success* (2019), Simon Sinek, *The Infinite Game* (2019), Nicholas Dancer, *Day In, Day Out: The Secret Power in Showing Up and Doing the Work* (2019), Jim McCormick, *The First-Time Manager* (2018), Ray Dalio, *Principles: Life and Work* (2017), Randy Clark, *The New Manager's Workbook: A Crash Course in Effective Management* (2016), Gino Wickman, *How to Be a Great Boss* (2016), and Simon Sinek, *Start with Why: How Great Leaders Inspire Everyone to Take Action* (2009). This is by no means an exhaustive list and each publication offers the reader valuable information on understanding issues related to today's manager.

Today's Manager

The roles and principles outlined in this publication present a singular focus on what the manager can do. Economist John Kenneth Galbraith noted: "conventional wisdom serves to protect us from the painful job of thinking."[6] The modern-day manager can ill afford to engage in conventional wisdom. The challenges are too significant, the issues too severe, and the questions too complex. Unfortunately, many managers hold a rather lackluster approach to managing. While managers generally welcome the status, rank, and privilege associated with the position, Teresa Amabile and Steve Kramer noted "many managers conceive of management quite narrowly—as focusing on organizational structure, short-term

---

[6] Galbraith, J.K. 1961. *The Great Crash, 1929*. Houghton Mifflin. https://google. com/books/edition/The_great_crash_1929/g04EAQAAIAAJ?hl=en

strategy, and the next quarter's profits but lack the belief managing serves a higher cause—the society and the people who constitute it."[7] As Peter Drucker proclaimed, "Management is so much more than exercising rank and privilege; it is much more than making deals. Management affects people and their lives."[8] But managing today must go beyond Drucker's observation. Managing in a volatile world requires a deep belief in the unique contributions of each employee, demands a recognition of each person's humanity, and mandates a dedication to grow both personally and professionally. Unfortunately, lack of training, delayed training, and being overwhelmed with administrative tasks are just three of the many reasons why managers lack the belief managing serves a higher cause.

Writing in *Forbes*, Victor Lipman observed that "companies with under 100 employees on average provide less than one hour (0.8 hour, or 48 minutes) of manager training per six-month period."[9] A study by West Monroe Partners found that among managers who oversee one to two employees, 59 percent report having no training at all; the same measure stands at 41 percent among those who oversee three to five workers.[10] Simply put, too many people who become first-time managers, or move up the management ladder, lack any formal training. Unfortunately, many people "tend to think management is something they are magically and automatically ready for when promoted or hired into the role."[11] If training does occur, it often takes

---

[7] As Amabile, T., and S. Kramer. 2011. "Horrible Bosses?" *Harvard Business Review*. Blog Post, July 18, 2011. https://hbr.org/2011/07/in-a-comment-on-our.html

[8] As Amabile, T., and S. Kramer. 2011. "Horrible Bosses?" *Harvard Business Review*. Blog Post, July 18, 2011. https://hbr.org/2011/07/in-a-comment-on-our.html

[9] Lipman, V. 2019. "Why Do So Many People Think Management doesn't Require Training?" *Forbes*, March 4, 2019. https://forbes.com/sites/victorlipman/2019/03/04/why-do-so-many-people-think-management-doesnt-require-training/#79cac9b06a8e

[10] "Companies are Overlooking a Primary Area for Growth and Efficiency: Their Managers." *Report, West Monroe Partners*, March 27, 2018. https://westmonroepartners.com/Insights/Newsletters/Productivity-Imperative

[11] Lipman, V. 2019. "Why do so Many People Think Management doesn't Require Training?" *Forbes*, March 4, 2019. https://forbes.com/sites/victorlipman/2019/03/04/why-do-so-many-people-think-management-doesnt-require-training/#79cac9b06a8e

place after someone has been in a management position for several years. According to the Association of Talent Development, "that's just too late! This delayed attention to training management skills can do real damage not only to individual careers, but also to organizational success."[12] "In addition to lack of training, managers often report they're too busy with administrative tasks to adequately oversee their team with 36 percent report spending up to four hours per day on administrative work. It's no surprise then 44 percent of managers frequently feel overwhelmed at work."[13] The end result of little or no training, a lack of understanding as to their role, and frequently feeling overwhelmed is the fact that a paltry 30 percent of employees feel engaged as reported by the Gallup organization.[14] This low employee engagement rating has existed for years and continues to serve as an illustration of managerial ineffectiveness. It's no wonder managers are often maligned in popular culture as evidenced in *The Devil Wears Prada, Horrible Bosses, The Office, Dilbert,* and *The Proposal.* Low employee engagement often has a negative impact on change management efforts undertaken by managers.

As David Michels wrote in *Forbes,* "The ability to successfully change—both as leaders and as organizations—is quickly becoming a source of competitive advantage."[15] An agile manager in a volatile world can expect constant change. The predicable managerial bliss of turning the lights on at 9:00 a.m. and shutting them off at 5:00 p.m. is no longer viable. According to research by the consulting firm Gartner, "The typical organization today has undertaken five major firm-wide changes in the past three years—and nearly 75 percent of organizations expect to multiply the types

---

[12] Blanchard, S. 2018. "Great Managers Aren't Born, They're Trained." *Association for Talent Development Insights,* April 18, 2018. https://td.org/insights/great-managers-arent-born-theyre-trained

[13] O'Donnell, R. 2018. "Managers say They Lack Training, and 44 % Feel Overwhelmed at Work." *HR Drive,* April 3, 2018. https://hrdive.com/news/managers-say-they-lack-training-and-44-feel-overwhelmed-at-work/520396/

[14] Gallup: U.S. Employee Engagement, https://news.gallup.com/poll/180404/gallup-daily-employee-engagement.aspx

[15] Michels, D. 2019. "Change is Changing: Coping with the Death of Traditional Change Management." *Forbes,* April 22, 2019. https://forbes.com/sites/davidmichels/2019/04/22/change-is-changing-coping-with-the-death-of-traditional-change-management/#7fad4d945308

of major change initiatives they will undertake in the next three years."[16] When it comes to change management, however, the ineffectiveness of a manager is striking. According to one research project 70 percent of business critical change efforts fail to achieve expected results due to poor leadership, inadequate management, weak rewards, and poor culture.[17] The first step in addressing managerial ineffectiveness is recognizing managers' lack the agility, resilience, and creativity required to keep pace with today's hyperconnected world. But this must change. Today's dynamic, ever-changing, and hypercompetitive global marketplace demands that managers increase their self-awareness and think differently. Small and medium-sized businesses, large corporations, nonprofits, and educational institutions at every level all need managers committed to creating the organizational change required to remain relevant, viable, and sustainable. As a manager in today's volatile world, it is imperative to realize the skills required to affect change are more complex, according to a report issued by The Center for Creative Leadership, and "involve a variety of competencies such as adaptability, self-awareness, boundary spanning, collaboration, and network thinking."[18] Perhaps the most important of these competencies for a manager to develop in today's volatile world is self-awareness.

Self-Awareness

The development of one's self-awareness is the foundation upon which a manager can increase their own agility, and in turn, help an organization do the same. Self-awareness is commonly defined as the capacity to focus attention on oneself and engage in periodic self-assessments. Doing so is the prerequisite to effectively affect the necessary change in an organization to achieve and sustain growth. In *True North: Discover Your Authentic Leadership*, authors Bill George and Peter Sims stated:

---

[16] "Managing Organizational Change: How HR Can Deliver on Complex Organizational Change Management Initiatives," Report, Gartner, https://gartner.com/en/human-resources/insights/organizational-change-management

[17] The Forum Corporation, 2015. "Developing Your Leaders." https://drive.google.com/file/d/1Y53pjgnbia4qVrueArYoKkHnRl6MCmgu/view?usp=sharing

[18] Petrie, N. 2014. "Future trends in Leadership Development." *The Center for Creative Leadership*. www.leanconstruction.org/media/learning_laboratory/Leadership/Future_Trends_in_Leadership_Development.pdf

"You must understand yourself, because the hardest person you will ever have to lead is yourself. Once you have an understanding of your authentic self, you will find that leading others is much easier."[19] Researchers Rasmus Hougaard, Jacqueline Carter, and Marissa Afton "conducted a survey of more than 1,000 leaders in more than 800 companies in over 100 countries, and found that leaders at the highest levels tend to have better self-awareness than leaders lower in the hierarchy."[20]

At first glance, it would appear self-awareness is an easy task to accomplish. People spend more time with themselves than they do with anyone else. Individuals, or in this case, managers, for example, are alone with their thoughts, feelings, and beliefs far more than they discuss such matters with others. A common misperception is the assumption that people possess a high level of self-awareness and know who they are. The evidence suggests otherwise. In her research, Tasha Eurich discovered just how glaring the lack of self-awareness is. According to Eurich, "even though most people believe they are self-aware, self-awareness is a truly rare quality with only 10%–15% of the people we studied actually fit the criteria."[21] As Peg O'Connor observed, "Knowing oneself is perhaps so difficult because we are simultaneously the inquirer and the object studied. It is difficult to get a good, right, or accurate perspective. Despite the difficulties in seeing oneself (literally and metaphorically), one must be able to do so."[22]

When one exerts efforts into improving their self-awareness, the research indicates confidence and creativity increases, decision making improves, communication enhances, and people are "more-effective leaders with

---

[19] George, B., and P. Sims. 2007. *True North: Discover Your Authentic Leadership.* Jossey-Bass, https://tinyurl.com/qov9j2v

[20] Hougaard, R., J. Carter, and M. Afton. 2018. "Self-Awareness can Help Leaders more than an MBA Can." *Harvard Business Review,* January 12, 2018. https://hbr.org/2018/01/self-awareness-can-help-leaders-more-than-an-mba-can

[21] Eurich, T. 2018. "What Self-Awareness Really is (and How to Cultivate it)." *Harvard Business Review,* January 4, 2018. https://hbr.org/2018/01/what-self-awareness-really-is-and-how-to-cultivate-it

[22] O'Connor, P. 2016. "Knowing How to Belong to Yourself." *Psychology Today,* December 14, 2016. https://psychologytoday.com/us/blog/philosophy-stirred-not-shaken/201612/knowing-how-belong-yourself

more-satisfied employees and more-profitable companies."[23] "Becoming a truly effective manager," writes Jennifer Stine of the Harvard Extension School, "requires a great deal of self-reflection, observation, and growth. The best managers I've seen have the ability to stay open to new information and experiences while also demonstrating strengths like empathy, inquiry, and emotional regulation."[24] Paul J. Silvia and Maureen E. O'Brian concluded "without self-awareness, people could not take the perspectives of others, exercise self-control, produce creative accomplishments, experience pride and high self-esteem" or navigate their own career development.[25]

Just as the agile manager needs to take a proactive role in managing their organization in a volatile world, so too much they take a similar approach when navigating their career. Robert S. Kaplan, emeritus professor of leadership development at the Harvard Business School stressed the need for self-awareness as it relates to career trajectory and observed "fulfillment doesn't come from clearing hurdles others set for you; it comes from clearing those you set for yourself."[26] Setting goals, creating a plan to accomplish them, and figuring out a way to navigate the chaos encountered while pursuing them are critical skills for the agile manager operating in a volatile world. Instead of allowing others to set hurdles for themselves, Kaplan understood that those who reached their potential set their own goals. Agile managers need to demonstrate the same level of heightened self-reliance. Moreover, Jonathan T. Mason acknowledged the essential role of self-awareness in career development and noted "career success and satisfaction will most likely be achieved by individuals who develop insights into themselves and their work environments."[27]

[23] Eurich, T. 2018. "What Self-Awareness Really is (and how to cultivate it)." *Harvard Business Review,* January 4, 2018. https://hbr.org/2018/01/what-self-awareness-really-is-and-how-to-cultivate-it

[24] Stine, J. "How Self-Awareness Makes you a Better Manager." *Harvard Extension School,* blog post, https://extension.harvard.edu/professional-development/blog/how-self-awareness-makes-you-better-manager

[25] Silvia, P.J., and M.E. O'Brien. 2004. "Self-Awareness and Constructive Functioning: Revisiting 'The Human Dilemma'". Journal of Social and Clinical Psychology 23, no. 4, 475–489. https://doi.org/10.1521/jscp.23.4.475.40307

[26] Kaplan, R.S. 2008. "Reaching Your Potential." *Harvard Business Review*, July–August 2008. https://hbr.org/2008/07/reaching-your-potential

[27] Mason, J.T. "Self-Awareness." *Career Research,* www.career.iresearchnet.com/career-development/self-awareness/

Remember, "self-knowledge is not a luxury but rather a necessity. Not having self-knowledge can lead to very hurtful, harmful, and even catastrophic consequences."[28] In today's volatile, uncertain, complex, and ambiguous global marketplace, organizations small and large can ill afford managers lacking self-knowledge.

Fortunately, the latest research indicates that organizations are placing more of a priority on self-awareness, skill development, and lifelong learning. This shift is a result of businesses realizing recent "college graduates often find themselves lacking both the technical and practical skills they need in their first jobs."[29] With colleges lagging behind in preparing students, organizations have taken it upon themselves to train employees more so than in the past. A 2020 Deloitte Insights report indicated a positive trend in training employees and found "one a fifth of executives completely agree that their organizations are currently ready, and just 10 percent said they are making a great deal of progress identifying, attracting, and retaining the right talent."[30] Instead of placing the onus of skill development and training on the employee through a college education, "over 80 percent of executives said they either have created or are creating a corporate culture of lifelong learning, with another 17 percent planning to do so."[31]

---

[28] O'Connor, P. 2016. "Knowing How to Belong to Yourself." *Psychology Today*, December 14, 2016. https://psychologytoday.com/us/blog/philosophy-stirred-not-shaken/201612/knowing-how-belong-yourself

[29] Wilkie, D. 2019. "Employers Say College Grads Lack Hard Skills, Too." *SHRM*, October 21, 2019. https://shrm.org/resourcesandtools/hr-topics/employee-relations/pages/employers-say-college-grads-lack-hard-skills-too.aspx

[30] "The Fourth Industrial Revolution: At the Intersection of Readiness and Responsibility." *Deloitte Insights*, 2020 https://www2.deloitte.com/content/dam/insights/us/articles/us32959-industry-4-0/DI_Industry4.0.pdf

[31] "The Fourth Industrial Revolution: At the Intersection of Readiness and Responsibility." *Deloitte Insights*, 2020. https://www2.deloitte.com/content/dam/insights/us/articles/us32959-industry-4-0/DI_Industry4.0.pdf

CHAPTER 1

The Six Functions of an Agile Manager

Today's manager would be unrecognizable to Henri Fayol (1841–1925), French mining engineer, executive, and author widely acknowledged as a founder of modern management method. In his original work, *General and Industrial Management: Planning, Organizing, Staffing, Directing, and Controlling*, Fayol identified five primary functions of the manager: planning, organizing, staffing, directing, and controlling. Those functions served managers well in the past when the marketplace was defined by risk, fear, and avoidance. In today's volatile global marketplace marked by constant disruption, Fayol's functions fall far short in providing the blueprint individuals need to succeed as managers. Today's hyperconnected global economy is defined by "possibility, agility and opportunity and requires managers to both manage and embrace change."[1] Doing so remains difficult for most people. As the American Management Association noted, "managers need to alter their thinking patterns and try new things to respond to change. They may be stuck in a rut, however, which makes it hard to meet today's challenges."[2]

Helping managers embrace agility involves updating Fayol's primary functions for today and identifying relevant principles for each function. Whereas Fayol's functions involved the verbs planning, organizing,

---

[1] Michels, D. 2019. "Change Is Changing: Coping With the Death Of Traditional Change Management." *Forbes*, April 22, 2019. https://forbes.com/sites/davidmichels/2019/04/22/change-is-changing-coping-with-the-death-of-traditional-change-management/#7fad4d945308

[2] "How Managers Can Shift Their Thinking and Respond to Change." *American Management Association*, August 8, 2018. https://playbook.amanet.org/training-articles-managers-change-thinking-patterns/

staffing, directing, and controlling, this publication relies on the nouns: curator, architect, conductor, humanist, advocate, and pioneer. This revision from verb to noun reflects the manager's need to shift their thinking from a position of status to one of perspective. This new way of thinking allows the manager to become more agile and understand their position is far more dynamic, empowering, and creative than previously considered. This new way of thinking will change the actual work managers do. And this new way of thinking is available to all managers, regardless of industry, position, title, training, budget, or educational background.

The six functions of an agile manager defined in this book are the following:

- *Curator*: gathers information, knowledge, and actionable intelligence
- *Architect*: conceptualizes, builds, and revises the operational blueprint
- *Conductor*: ensures collaboration, skill development, and harmony
- *Humanist*: emphasizes the value and agency of human beings
- *Advocate*: communicates the mission, values, and vision
- *Pioneer*: explores new ideas, products, and services

The first function of an agile manager is that of a curator studying the information, knowledge, and actionable intelligence required to comprehend the attributes of today's global marketplace. Understanding today's dynamic, hyperconnected, and ever-changing landscape can help a manager grasp the disruptive forces impacting the organization (Principle #1). Surveying the landscape involves defining the Fourth Industrial Revolution, examining the impact of hyperconnectivity, and studying the characteristics of a volatile, uncertain, complex, and ambiguous (VUCA) environment. Knowledge of change attributes will allow an individual to self-reflect on the risks associated with their ability to develop as an agile manager (Principle #2). The risk of conventional thinking, the risk of lacking a decision-making process, and the risk of remaining comfortable all pose credible threats to becoming an agile manager. Once risks are identified, the manager needs to assess their ability to ask the relevant questions required to help move the organization forward. (Principle #3). Engaging in double-loop learning, encouraging people to ask questions, and exploring answers to questions all play a central role in the agile manager's ability to ask relevant questions.

The second function of an agile manager is that of an architect. This function allows the manager to create or update an organization's mission to remain relevant (Principle #4). As retired U.S. Army general Eric Ken Shinseki said: "If you dislike change, you're going to dislike irrelevance even more."[3] Managers looking to develop their agility should heed Shinseki's words closely. Technological disruptions continue to alter the very fabric of life and work so a review of an organization's mission statement is only prudent for the agile manager. Upon review of the mission, the agile manager can work toward designing the vision of an organization (Principle #5). Designing a vision will allow the agile manager to maintain an organization's focus while navigating the chaos of a volatile world. Once the mission is reviewed and updated if necessary and the vision designed, an agile manager can cultivate the values of an organization's culture (Principle #6). The values drive the expectations, behaviors, and attitudes of employees and help the organization maintain consistency of work across departments and functional areas.

The third function of an agile manager is that of a conductor ensuring collaboration, skill development, and harmony among internal constituents and between the organization and external stakeholders and partners. Fostering collaboration across departments, functional areas, and offices illustrates a critical component of agility (Principle #7). Managers also need to demonstrate a commitment to ensuring employees receiving the skill development, training, and education required to succeed (Principle #8). Such collaboration and skill development prepares the organization to navigate the dynamics of a volatile global marketplace as the agile manager nurtures relationships with external stakeholders (Principle #9).

The fourth function of an agile manager is that of a humanist who emphasizes the value and agency of human beings, individually and

---

[3] Eric Shinseki, Wikipedia, https://en.wikiquote.org/wiki/Eric_Shinseki

collectively. The human capital needs of today demand agile managers establish a humanist culture based on diversity, equity, and inclusion (Principle #10). An appreciation of the unique qualities of each person will help the agile manager better understand how to build productive teams (Principle #11). Demonstrating compassion, kindness, and empathy are often understated in the role of management but remain a critical tenet of the agile manager in a volatile world (Principle #12).

The fifth function of an agile manager is that of an advocate promoting the work, employees, and value of the organization as it looks to break through the inordinate amount of noise in the marketplace. Creating content on a regular basis will help the agile manager promote the work of the organization (Principle #13). Telling stories about the people who work there can help the organization relate to customers, partners, and suppliers (Principle #14). The manager then needs to diversify the distribution of both the content and stories to as many social media platforms and outlets as possible (Principle #15).

The sixth function of an agile manager is that of a pioneer exploring new ideas for products and services that inspire employees and customers alike. An agile manager should encourage dialogue from employees and others about the organization's products and services (Principle #16). During the dialogue, an agile manager should remain opened minded about new ideas (Principle #17). This encouragement of open dialogue and consideration of new ideas can help the agile manager inspire others as the organization looks to move forward in today's volatile world (Principle #18).

CHAPTER 2

The Agile Manager's Self-Assessment

Agility: Management Principles for A Volatile World offers the manager a self-assessment designed to increase self-awareness. As Gallup noted, "You cannot have a culture of agility until you equip your managers with the right development, clear expectations, ongoing coaching and accountability."[1] Since "self-awareness involves being clear on personal values, understanding strengths and weaknesses, and being cognizant of one's impact on others," frequent self-assessments play an important role for the agile manager.[2] Elena Bothelho and Kim Powell published *The CEO Next Door: The 4 Behaviors That Transform Ordinary People into World-Class Leaders* and discussed how their research emphasized the role of self-assessments and self-awareness for top executives. The four behaviors of world-class leaders are the following:

- *Decide*: speed over precision
- *Engage for impact*: orchestrate stakeholders to drive results
- *Relentless reliability*: deliver consistently
- *Adapt boldly*: ride the discomfort of the unknown

---

[1] Clifton, J., and J. Harter. 2019. "It's the Manager: From Gallup, Based on the Largest Global Study on the Future of Work." *SlideShare* presentation dated June 16, 2019. https://slideshare.net/ShivShivakumar1/book-summary-its-the-manager

[2] *Data Driven: What Students Need to Succeed in a Rapidly Changing Business World.* PwC white paper dated February 2015. https://cpb-us-w2.wpmucdn.com/sites.gsu.edu/dist/1/1670/files/2015/08/pwc-data-driven-paper-1wdb00u.pdf

Bothelho and Powell noted, "there is no perfect, all-weather leader at any level who excels at all four of the behaviors."[3] The agile manager in a volatile world should worry less about being perfect and spend more time practicing the art of being nimble. The demands of today's hypercompetitive global marketplace will challenge even the most seasoned manager. As such, note that world-class leaders achieved their proficiency in each of the four areas over a period of time involving a good deal of self-reflection, "identifying where they were weak and working to build strength over time."[4] Just as the development of an agile organization happens over time, so too does the maturation of an agile manager.

For those agile managers new to the concept of reflection time and self-assessment know that both are invaluable for CEOs as well as employees at any level. In their paper "Making Experience Count: The Role of Reflection in Individual Learning," Giada Di Stefano and colleagues concluded, "employees who spent 15 minutes at the end of the day reflecting about lessons learned performed 23 percent better after 10 days than those who did not reflect."[5] On the other hand, if a manager refuses to find time for reflection and complete self-assessments, they will miss opportunities to grow both personally and professionally. As one executive coach noted, "the hardest leaders to coach are those who won't reflect; particularly leaders who won't reflect on themselves."[6] But the resistance to reflection seems to have met its match now that employers

---

[3] Bothelho, E., and K. Powell. 2017. *The CEO Next Door: The 4 Behaviors that Transform Ordinary People into World-Class Leaders.* Penguin Random House. https://tinyurl.com/toltefq

[4] Elena Bothelho and Kim Powell. 2017. *The CEO Next Door: The 4 Behaviors that Transform Ordinary People into World-Class Leaders.* Penguin Random House. https://tinyurl.com/toltefq

[5] Giada Di Stefano, Francesca Gino, Gary Pisano, and Bradley Staats, "Making Experience Count: The Role of Reflection in Individual Learning, Harvard Business School NOM Unit Working Paper No. 14-093Harvard Business School Technology & Operations Mgt. Unit Working Paper No. 14-093HEC Paris Research Paper No. SPE-2016-1181. https://papers.ssrn.com/sol3/papers.cfm?abstract_id=2414478

[6] Jennifer Porter, "Why You Should Make Time for Self-Reflection (Even If You Hate Doing It)," *Harvard Business Review*, March 21, 2017. https://hbr.org/2017/03/why-you-should-make-time-for-self-reflection-even-if-you-hate-doing-it

are conducting personality assessments on new hires. Since organizations like "the apparel company Patagonia begin scrutinizing job applicants as soon as they walk through the door for interviews," it behooves the agile manager to incorporate reflection in their routine to know who they are before someone else tells them.[7]

Prior to completing the following Agile Manager's Self-Assessment, keep in mind the following ten components of reflection.

1. This self-assessment is available to everyone regardless of level, function, or title. This self-assessment is free and requires a small amount of time so it can be completed without interfering with the normal course of a workday. The manager looking to increase their organization's agility should, however, demonstrate by example, and discuss the value of completing the self-assessment to employees.

2. Agility should be on everyone's performance plan if the organization is to achieve any degree of nimbleness to compete more effectively. Agility or irrelevance—therein lies the choice for organizations today from local small businesses, to medium-sized companies, to large corporations. Therefore, agility should find its way onto everyone's performance plan.

3. This self-assessment could be used in conjunction with the other performance measurements outlined by the manager. For example, if a salesperson has a goal of acquiring five new clients that in and of itself is a performance measurement; but so too is the salesperson's agility as measured by this self-assessment.

4. This self-assessment should be used on a regular basis. At a minimum, the manager should conduct this assessment each quarter, although monthly would most likely offer a better trend over time analysis. Quarterly gives a manager four snap shots in a 12-month period while monthly provides 12 observations into their behavior.

5. The first time someone completes the assessment it may take a bit longer since their familiarity with the six functions may be limited.

---

[7] Sue Shellenbarger, "The Best Bosses Are Humble Bosses," *The Wall Street Journal,* October 9, 2018. https://www.wsj.com/articles/the-best-bosses-are-humble-bosses-1539092123

Over time, as the six functions are discussed on a more frequent basis, the self-assessment should be completed with greater ease. In the ideal situation, teams would get together and discuss some operational issue and incorporate the six functions right into the conversation. Doing so would resemble an assessment in real time so they understand just how agile they are at that moment.

6. Be focused over the long term. It is important to track the self-assessments conducted over time as they will offer a tremendous source of reflection material. This self-assessment makes it simply for one to focus on agility as there are only six functions. If need be, one can focus their attention on one function at a time and measure that during some predetermined period of time, a week for example.

7. Be open-ended as there are no right or wrong answers. The point of the self-assessment is to identify how often one practiced the six functions of the agile manager. There is no grade associated with this self-assessment.

8. Remember the Situation, Task, Action, Result (STAR) format. Agile managers can ask themselves questions such as:
   a. What situations were challenging?
   b. What tasks helped address the situation?
   c. What activities or actions were required to accomplish each task?
   d. What were the results of those actions on the organization's mission or goals?

As one completes the self-assessment, they should like their STAR examples to a specific function for greater clarity. For example, the first function of the agile manager is curator. What recent situation did the manager face that required them to function as a curator? Did they? If they did, they what tasks did they accomplish? What activities did they take? What were the results?

9. Be kind. Self-assessments done carelessly can open wounds. The agile manager operating in a volatile world needs to remind themselves to be kind. This kindness needs to be extended to themselves as well as to any employee willing to undergo the self-assessment. Perfection is far from the goal here. Practice. That in and of itself is the goal. Practice becoming more agile. Practice remaining open-minded. And practice the six functions of the agile manager as much

as possible knowing full well it is impossible to work at the highest levels for each one all of the time.

10. Managing people will invariably involve dealing with unforeseen external events that place tremendous stress on the organization. The COVID-19 global pandemic is one such example. During such times of extreme stress, this self-assessment can serve as a reminder of the functions most important for the organization to leverage to navigate the chaos of the event. As one observer noted, "Adapting to change will be our new normal and companies need to be agile. The Coronavirus (COVID-19) crisis has brought big, unprecedented challenges that require companies to respond to a new business environment."[8]

The Agile Manager's Self-Assessment Template

Directions: Assess how often you practiced each of the six functions of the agile manager using the Likert scale of: never, sometimes, often, frequently, and always.

Time period: _____ Date: _____

The Agile Manager's Self-Assessment						
	Curator	Architect	Conductor	Humanist	Advocate	Pioneer
Always						
Frequently						
Often						
Sometimes						
Never						

In a given week never means 0 days; sometimes means 1 day; often means 2–3 days, frequently means 4–5 days, and always means 7 days.

Notes:

Examples of notes include those situations, actions, tasks, and results related to one or more of the six functions.

---

[8] "Agile in the Age of COVID-19," *HRCI Team*, April 21, 2020. https://hrci.org/community/blogs-and-announcements/hr-leads-business-blog/hr-leads-business/2020/04/21/agile-in-the-age-of-covid-19

The Agile Manager's Self-Assessment Example

Directions: Assess how often you practiced each of the six functions of the agile manager using the Likert scale of: never, sometimes, often, frequently, and always.

Time period: *During the last week* Date: May 2, 2020

The Agile Manager's Self-Assessment						
	Curator	Architect	Conductor	Humanist	Advocate	Pioneer
Always						
Frequently					X	
Often		X		X		
Sometimes	X		X			X
Never						

In a given week never means 0 days; sometimes means 1 day; often means 2–3 days, frequently means 4–5 days, and always means 7 days.

Notes:

During the last week, I sometimes performed the function of curator. There were opportunities for me to function as a curator, but other obligations required my time, effort, and commitment.

During the last week I frequently performed the function of an advocate. A local television channel invited me to be a part of a panel of local managers. Therefore, a good deal of my time Monday and Tuesday of this week was preparing for this advocate function.

CHAPTER 3

Curator

Introduction to Function #1: Curator

The first function of an agile manager is that of a curator studying the information, knowledge, and actionable intelligence required to comprehend the attributes of today's global marketplace. Understanding today's dynamic, hyperconnected, 9 and ever-changing landscape can help a manager grasp the disruptive forces impacting the organization (Principle #1). Surveying the landscape involves defining the Fourth Industrial Revolution, examining the impact of hyperconnectivity, and studying the characteristics of a volatile, uncertain, complex, and ambiguous (VUCA) environment. Knowledge of change attributes will allow an individual to self-reflect on the risks associated with their ability to develop as an agile manager (Principle #2). The risk of conventional thinking, lacking a decision-making process, and remaining comfortable all pose credible threats to becoming an agile manager. Once risks are identified, the manager needs to assess their ability to ask the relevant questions required to help move the organization forward (Principle #3). Engaging in double-loop learning, encouraging people to ask questions, and exploring answers to questions all play a central role in the agile manager's ability to ask relevant questions.

Understanding the landscape, identifying risks, and asking questions are three principles that can help the agile manager perform the function of a curator studying information, knowledge, and actionable intelligence. In his 1753 publication *On the Interpretation of Nature*, French philosopher Denis Diderot wrote, "There are three principal means of acquiring knowledge available to us: observation of nature, reflection, and experimentation. Observation collects facts; reflection combines them;

experimentation verifies the result of that combination."[1] Although some 270 plus years old, Diderot's explanation of acquiring knowledge remains relevant, especially for agile managers seeking to perform the function of a curator. Diderot continued and wrote, "Our observation of nature must be diligent, our reflection profound, and our experiments exact. We rarely see these three means combined; and for this reason, creative geniuses are not common." While a creative genius may be an unnecessary pursuit for an agile manager in a volatile world, diligent observations, profound reflections, and exact experiments are certainly necessary tasks. Thus, the first principle of the agile manager in a volatile world is understanding the landscape.

Principle Number 1: Understand the Landscape

Understanding today's dynamic, hyperconnected, and ever-changing landscape can help a manager grasp the disruptive forces impacting the organization (Principle #1). Surveying the landscape involves defining the Fourth Industrial Revolution, examining the impact of hyperconnectivity, and studying the characteristics of a VUCA environment. Coined by Klaus Schwab, founder and executive chairman of the World Economic Forum, and the title of his 2017 book *The Fourth Industrial Revolution*, he explains how today's disruptive technologies blur the lines between the physical, digital, and biological spheres. A 2020 Deloitte Insights report identified the Fourth Industrial Revolution as Industry 4.0 and defined it as "the marriage of physical assets and advanced digital technologies—the Internet of Things (IoT), artificial intelligence (AI), robots, drones, autonomous vehicles, 3D printing, cloud computing, nanotechnology, and more—that communicate, analyze, and act upon information enabling organizations, consumers, and society to be more flexible and responsive and make more intelligent, data-driven decisions."[2] These technological changes are drastically altering how individuals, companies, and govern-

---

[1] Denis Diderot, Wikiquote, https://en.wikiquote.org/wiki/Denis_Diderot

[2] "The Fourth Industrial Revolution: At the Intersection of Readiness and Responsibility." *Deloitte Insights*, 2020. https://www2.deloitte.com/content/dam/insights/us/articles/us32959-industry-4-0/DI_Industry4.0.pdf

ments operate, ultimately leading to a societal transformation similar to previous industrial revolutions.[3] Sue Bhatia echoed similar sentiment in a February 20, 2020, *Forbes* article and wrote: "We are in the midst of a revolution. It is one of such immensity that the changes it is set to bring will be epic."[4]

Following is an abbreviated outline of the four industrial revolutions:

- First Industrial Revolution: 1765–1865
    ○ Steam engines and railroads.
- Second Industrial Revolution: 1865–1965
    ○ Mass production, automobiles, steel, and the telephone.
- Third Industrial Revolution: 1965–2015
    ○ Nuclear energy, electronics, telecommunications, computers and the Internet.
- Fourth Industrial Revolution: 2015 to present
    ○ Artificial intelligence, autonomous vehicles, drones, and the Internet of Things.

The Third Industrial Revolution launched global connectivity through the creation of email in the 1960s, file sharing since the 1970s, and the invention of the first web browser by English scientist Tim Berners-Lee in 1991. The number of people online skyrocketed from half percent in 1991 to 413 million in 2000 and over 3.4 billion by 2016, making the Internet one of the most transformative and fast-growing technologies in world history.[5] As explained on the World Economic Forum web site, "The Fourth Industrial Revolution represents a fundamental change in the way we live, work and relate to one another. It is a new chapter in human development, enabled by extraordinary technology advances commen-

---

[3] Schulze, E. 2019. "Everything you Need to know About the Fourth Industrial Revolution." *CNBC*, January 17, 2019. https://cnbc.com/2019/01/16/fourth-industrial-revolution-explained-davos-2019.html

[4] Bhatia, S. 2020. "The Fourth Industrial Revolution is Changing Work." *Forbes*, February 20, 2020. https://forbes.com/sites/forbesbusinessdevelopmentcouncil/2020/02/20/the-fourth-industrial-revolution-is-changing-work/#58188623a220

[5] Roser, M., H. Ritchie, and E. Ortiz-Ospina. 2020. "Internet." *Published online at OurWorldInData.org.* https://ourworldindata.org/internet

surate with those of the first, second and third industrial revolutions."[6] Since "digital technology is so intertwined with many businesses, as well as our social and economic lives, trying to separate 'tech' from 'non-tech' is becoming increasingly redundant," said David Stubbs, head of client investment strategy for EMEA at J.P. Morgan Private Bank.[7] Despite the preponderance of change in today's Fourth Industrial Revolution, traditional mindsets and "that's the way we've always done it around here" (cultural attitude) are the two biggest primary culprits hindering the fundamental transformation emerging technologies are meant to enable.[8] Commenting on this new era of disruptive technologies responsible for launching the Fourth Industrial Revolution, *New York Times* columnist Thomas Friedman wrote: "globalization and the information technology revolution have gone to a whole new level. Thanks to cloud computing, robotics, 3G wireless connectivity, Skype, Facebook, Google, LinkedIn, Twitter, the iPad, and cheap Internet-enabled smartphones, the world has gone from connected to hyper-connected."[9]

During the last four years, the number of people connected around the world continued to increase. In its 2020 report, HootSuite noted of the 7.7 billion people around the world, 5.2 billion (67 percent) have a mobile phone and 4.5 (59 percent) have access to the Internet and 3.8 billion (49 percent) are active social media users. The levels of global adoption for other technologies also escalated during the last two decades. For example, mobile phones took 12 years to reach 50 million users while the Internet took just seven to get to the same point. "Looking at purely digital technologies, the rates become frantic: Facebook reached 50 million users in four years;

[6] World Economic Forum. "The Fourth Industrial Revolution." https://weforum.org/focus/fourth-industrial-revolution

[7] Schulze, E. 2017. "Everything you Need to Know About the Fourth Industrial Revolution." *CNBC*, January 17, 2019. https://cnbc.com/2019/01/16/fourth-industrial-revolution-explained-davos-2019.html

[8] Ibarra, H. Winter 2020. "Take a Wrecking Ball to Your Company's Iconic Practices." *Sloan Review*, https://sloanreview.mit.edu/article/take-a-wrecking-ball-to-your-companys-iconic-practices/

[9] Friedman, T.L. 2011. "A Theory of Everything (sort of)." *The New York Times*, August 13, 2011, https://nytimes.com/2011/08/14/opinion/sunday/Friedman-a-theory-of-everyting-sort-of.html

WeChat, one year. Pokémon GO, the augmented-reality gaming app from Niantic? Nineteen days."[10] These levels of global penetration rates illustrate very clearly how the world went from the connected to the hyperconnected during the last few years. While the pace may slow over the next decade, millions will come online for the first time each year. In 2019, for example, almost 300 million people came online for the first time; with the majority of those new users living in developing economies. As perhaps the strongest indication that the Internet is playing an ever more important role in our lives the world's Internet users spend an average of 6 hours and 43 minutes online each day.[11] This hyperconnectedness of billions of people around the globe has altered the very fabric of how humans do almost everything today.

Louis Rossetto, founder and former editor-in-chief of *Wired* magazine, summed it all up this way: "Digital technology is so broad today as to encompass almost everything. No product is made today, no person moves today, nothing is collected, analyzed or communicated without some 'digital technology' being an integral part of it."[12] Additionally, Larry Irving, cofounder of The Mobile Alliance for Global Good, wrote, "There is almost no area in which digital technology has not impacted me and my family's life."[13] Moreover, the 2019 Technology Vision survey of 6,672 business and IT executives found that 45 percent reported the "pace of innovation in their organizations has significantly accelerated over the past three years due to emerging technologies."[14] Hyperconnect-

[10] "Are You Ready For What's Next?" *Accenture Technology Vision 2019*. https://accenture.com/_acnmedia/pdf-94/accenture-techvision-2019-tech-trends-report.pdf

[11] "Essential Insights into How People Around The World Use The Internet, Mobile Devices, Social Media, and E-Commerce." *HootSuite*, 2020. https://p.widencdn.net/1zybur/Digital2020Global_Report_en

[12] Anderson, J., and L. Rainie. 2018. "The Positives of Digital Life." *Pew Research Center*, July 3, 2018. https://pewresearch.org/internet/2018/07/03/the-positives-of-digital-life/

[13] Anderson, J., and L. Rainie. 2018. "The Positives of Digital Life." *Pew Research Center*, July 3, 2018. https://pewresearch.org/internet/2018/07/03/the-positives-of-digital-life/

[14] "Are You Ready For What's Next?" *Accenture Technology Vision 2019*. https://accenture.com/_acnmedia/pdf-94/accenture-techvision-2019-tech-trends-report.pdf

edness has revolutionized the world and contributed to "groundbreaking changes in transportation, industry, communication, education, energy, health care, communication, entertainment, government, warfare and even basic research."[15]

"The average US adult will spend 3 hours, 43 minutes (referenced as 3:43) on mobile devices in 2019, just above the 3:35 spent on TV. Of time spent on mobile, US consumers will spend 2:55 on smartphones, a 9-minute increase from last year. In 2018, mobile time spent was 3:35, with TV time spent at 3:44."[16] Mobile applications have introduced person-to-person payments. Nonexistent prior to 2010, person-to-person payments made through a mobile device is expected to reach $336 billion by 2021.[17] Disruptive technologies were responsible for the music industry's decline in total global revenues from $23.9 billion in 2001 to $14.3 billion in 2014. Due to new services such as streaming digital music, the industry is experiencing an increase in global revenue and has steadily increased back up to $19.1 billion in 2018.[18]

The end result of hyperconnectedness and changing landscape, people's expectations change. In today's hyperconnected environment, "demand is communicated instantly, and gratification is expected immediately. What's more, both are constantly changing, creating an infinite and never-ending stream of opportunities to be met through business-to-business (B2B) and business-to-consumer (B2C) engagement."[19]

[15] Stansberry, K., J. Anderson, and L. Rainie. 2019. "The Internet Will Continue to Make Life Better." *Pew Research Center* October 28, 2019. https://pewresearch.org/internet/2019/10/28/4-the-internet-will-continue-to-make-life-better/

[16] He, A. 2019. "Average US time Spent with Mobile in 2019 has Increased Us Adults Spend More Time on Mobile than they do Watching TV." June 4, 2019, eMarketer, https://emarketer.com/content/average-us-time-spent-with-mobile-in-2019-has-increased

[17] Crosman, P. 2019. "10 Ways Technology Will Change Banking in 2019." *American Banker*, https://americanbanker.com/list/10-ways-technology-will-change-banking-in-2019

[18] IFPI Global Music Report, 2019. https://ifpi.org/news/IFPI-GLOBAL-MUSIC-REPORT-2019&lang=en

[19] "Are You Ready for What's Next?" *Accenture Technology Vision 2019*. https://accenture.com/_acnmedia/pdf-94/accenture-techvision-2019-tech-trends-report.pdf

Agile managers need to understand that "technology is the fabric of reality, and companies can use it to meet people wherever they are, at any moment in time—if they rise to the challenge."[20] "By positioning themselves as the curators of reality, companies already have a new level of obligation to society. But being able to deliver for specific and constantly changing moments creates challenging additional questions for businesses that are used to one market of many and long-static circumstances."[21] Tracy Wolstencroft, chief executive officer of global executive-search firm Heidrick & Struggles, noted this constantly changing environment and said, "we live in a *VUCA* world—volatility, uncertainty, complexity, and ambiguity where there's only room for humility. There is simply too much happening every given day that can make you humble. So, get ready for it. Be comfortable. Be comfortable being humble in a VUCA world."[22]

As Sunnie Giles wrote in *Forbes*, "VUCA is a concept that originated with students at the U.S. Army War College to describe the volatility, uncertainty, complexity, and ambiguity of the world after the Cold War.[23] Before proceeding let's define each word:

- Volatile: rate of change
- Uncertainty: unclear about the present
- Complexity: multiple key decision factors
- Ambiguity: lack of clarity about meaning of an event

---

[20] "Are You Ready for What's Next?" *Accenture Technology Vision 2019*. https://accenture.com/_acnmedia/pdf-94/accenture-techvision-2019-tech-trends-report.pdf

[21] "Are You Ready for What's Next?" *Accenture Technology Vision 2019*. https://accenture.com/_acnmedia/pdf-94/accenture-techvision-2019-tech-trends-report.pdf

[22] "Heidrick & Struggles on the Changing nature of Leadership." June 2015. Interview, McKinsey https://mckinsey.com/featured-insights/leadership/heidrick-and-struggles-on-the-changing-nature-of-leadership

[23] Giles, S. 2018. "How VUCA is Reshaping the Business Environment, and What It Means for Innovation." *Forbes*, May 9, 2018. https://forbes.com/sites/sunniegiles/2018/05/09/how-vuca-is-reshaping-the-business-environment-and-what-it-means-for-innovation/#7911de57eb8d

Regardless of experience, managers operating in a volatile world have an obligation to their self, employees, and organization to develop the skills, traits, and habits required to become agile. As Jim Kean, CEO of Steelcase, U.S. said "The role of the company is to continually challenge and develop its people, starting at the top. In fact, I think the company has an obligation to do so. You have to create a culture of learning. Investing in people and helping them continually develop their skills should be embedded in a company's culture."[24] Unfortunately this is more aspirational than institutional. According to Oxford Economics *Workforce 2020* report, "only 41% of employees say their company offers them opportunities to expand their skill sets."[25] More needs to be done here if organizations are going to remain relevant. Doing so is far more difficult than most managers understand. Even the "best and the brightest" managers and the "top companies" struggle with remaining relevant in today's volatile world. "The sad news is that very few organizations are prepared to operate in this higher level of complexity."[26] Evidence of this decline of relevant organizations once considered great was presented by Chris Bradley in his analysis of organizations listed in Tom Peters' 1982 book *In Search of Excellence*, and Jim Collins' 1994 *Built to Last* and 2001 *Good to Great*. Bradley discovered just how volatile the global marketplace is and concluded:

- Two well-performing companies were acquired (Amoco bought by BP and Gillette by P&G).
- Four low performers were swallowed up (Amdahl, Data General, DEC and Raychem).
- Three went bust (Kmart, Wang, and Circuit City).
- Another five fell off the list including Kodak's bankruptcy in 2013.

---

[24] PWC. 2020. "Navigating the Rising Tide of Uncertainty." 23rd Annual Global CEO Survey, February 2020. https://pwc.com/gx/en/ceo-survey/2020/reports/pwc-23rd-global-ceo-survey.pdf

[25] Oxford Economics, "Workforce 2020: The Looming Talent Crisis." 2020. https://tinyurl.com/tpunwq9

[26] Giles, S. 2018. "How VUCA is Reshaping the Business Environment, and What It Means for Innovation." *Forbes*, May 9, 2018. https://forbes.com/sites/sunniegiles/2018/05/09/how-vuca-is-reshaping-the-business-environment-and-what-it-means-for-innovation/#7911de57eb8d

Commenting on the volatility of the modern business world, and what, if anything, managers should do, Bradley wrote "above all, respect the trend, do everything you can to get ahead of it, and don't kid yourself that you can fight it. Even the greatest companies could not hold back the tide."[27] Options for agile managers include planning various scenarios, developing sophisticated financial projections, and dedicating significant time toward training the organization to become more agile. Much like a tsunami warning system (TWS) is used to detect tsunamis in advance and issue warnings to prevent loss of life and damage to property, so too must agile managers detect upcoming changes and help the organization think differently and create the organizational change required to achieve and sustain growth.[28] An organization's vitality, vibrancy, and relevance is directly related to the manager's ability to foster a more agile culture. Spencer Fung, Group CEO of Li & Fung, Hong Kong SAR, China, commented on the pace of change, the uncertainty in geopolitics, and the rearrangement of global supply chains stating "there's no way anybody can predict what's going to happen in five years. The uncertainty we see today is unprecedented in the last 40 years."[29] Commenting on the volumes of research and analysis available to managers predicting success by following a formula that specific actions will lead to predictable outcomes, Phil Rosenzweig noted, "The truth is very different: the business world is not a place of clear causal relationships, where a given set of actions leads to predictable results, but one that is more tenuous and uncertain."[30]

---

[27] Bradley, C. 2017. "Surprise: Those 'Great" Companies Generally Turn out to be Meh...or Duds." *MarketWatch*, August 31, 2017. https://marketwatch.com/story/great-companies-are-more-likely-to-do-really-badly-over-time-than-really-well-2017-07-12

[28] Wikipedia. "Tsunami Warning Systems." https://en.wikipedia.org/wiki/Tsunami_warning_system

[29] PWC. 2020. "Navigating the Rising Tide of Uncertainty," 23rd Annual Global CEO Survey, February 2020. https://pwc.com/gx/en/ceo-survey/2020/reports/pwc-23rd-global-ceo-survey.pdf

[30] Rosenzweig, P. 2007. "The Halo Effect, and Other Managerial Delusions." *McKinsey Quarterly*, February 2007. https://mckinsey.com/business-functions/strategy-and-corporate-finance/our-insights/the-halo-effect-and-other-managerial-delusions

Companies, governments, and organizations in the United States and around the world are struggling to keep up with the unprecedented pace of technological change. Only the agile will survive. Siemens is one example. With more than 1,500 open jobs in the United States alone, CEO of Siemens, U.S., Barbara Humpton highlighted her organization's agility and said, "We're making the human–machine interface more fluid and intuitive, because our current approach can't continue. So we're going to be training a lot of non-engineers to do jobs engineers would have done in the past."[31] In a January 2020 interview, CEO of PepsiCo Foods Mexico Roberto Martínez noted his agility and said, "From 2006 to now, we have reduced our water consumption in Mexico by 50%, and we're continuing that progress by investing in some very modern technologies. One is aeroponics, in which plants basically grow in the air, rather than in the earth. This allows us to consume a mere 10% of the amount of water compared to traditional agriculture."[32]

While examples of managerial agility like Martinez do exist, they are the exception more than the norm as "companies are ill-prepared for the leadership challenges of workforce 2020, and are not doing enough to meet future demands."[33] For those managers clinging to some make believe past who are hesitant to become agile because they believe things will go back to normal, make no mistake today's VUCA environment will only continue to affect change. "The revolution is coming in waves, so incremental changes may only be apparent at first. But rest assured there will be no part of the world of work that is left untouched. Companies that are unprepared for these changes will struggle in the revolution's wake."[34] Professor Günter Stahl and colleagues in

[31] PWC. 2020. "Navigating the Rising Tide of Uncertainty." *23rd Annual Global CEO Survey*, February 2020. https://pwc.com/gx/en/ceo-survey/2020/reports/pwc-23rd-global-ceo-survey.pdf

[32] Flores, A.P. 2020. "Using Technology to Rewire a Food Business." *Strategy + Business*, January 15, 2020. https://strategy-business.com/article/Using-technology-to-rewire-a-food-business?gko=444e7

[33] Oxford Economics. 2020. "Workforce 2020: The Looming Talent Crisis." 2020. https://tinyurl.com/tpunwq9

[34] Bhatia, S. 2020. "The Fourth Industrial Revolution is Changing Work." *Forbes*, February 20, 2020. https://forbes.com/sites/forbesbusinessdevelopmentcouncil/2020/02/20/the-fourth-industrial-revolution-is-changing-work/#58188623a220

the *MIT Sloan Management Review* noted, "Not only do businesses need to adjust to shifting demographics and workforce preferences, but they must also build new capabilities and revitalize their organizations—all while investing in new technologies, globalizing their operations, and contending with new competitors."[35] To delay agile practices could result in a loss of customers. Believe it or not, customers know they have other choices. "The research shows about half of customers say most companies fall short of their expectations for great experiences, while 76% report that it's easier than ever to take their business elsewhere."[36] The attributes of today's Fourth Industrial Revolution marked by hyperconnectedness and a VUCA environment is "changing rapidly, and any organism that doesn't change as fast the environment faces extinction."[37] To ensure an organization remains relevant, vibrant, and profitable, an agile manager understands the landscape (Principle #1) and learns to identify the risks (Principle #2) of managing in a volatile world.

Principle Number 2: Identify Risks

Identifying risks is the second principle of the agile manager looking to improve their function as a curator in today's volatile world. In his 2013 book *How to Fail at Almost Everything and Still Win Big: Kind of the Story of My Life*, cartoonist Scott Adams who created *Dilbert* highlights two important aspects of his success: "Good ideas have no value because the world already has too many of them. The market rewards execution, not ideas" and "Goals are for losers. Focus on the process." This later part applies to principle number 2: identify risks. After understanding

---

[35] Stahl, et. al. Winter 2012. "Six Principles of Effective Global Talent Management." *Sloan Review,* https://sloanreview.mit.edu/article/six-principles-of-effective-global-talent-management/

[36] McGinnis, D. 2018. "What is the Fourth Industrial Revolution." December 20, 2018. https://salesforce.com/blog/2018/12/what-is-the-fourth-industrial-revolution-4IR.html

[37] Giles, S. 2018. "How VUCA is Reshaping the Business Environment, and What It Means for Innovation." *Forbes*, May 9, 2018. https://forbes.com/sites/sunniegiles/2018/05/09/how-vuca-is-reshaping-the-business-environment-and-what-it-means-for-innovation/#7911de57eb8d

the landscape (Principle #1), the agile manager needs to have a process to identify risks (Principle #2). The two categories of risks managers are often told to identify are external and internal. External risks are macro-economic in nature and occur outside of the organization. The manager has absolutely no control over them. *The World Economic Forum Global Risks Report 2020* concluded: "The global economy is facing an increased risk of stagnation, climate change is striking harder and more rapidly than expected, and fragmented cyberspace threatens the full potential of next-generation technologies—all while citizens worldwide protest political and economic conditions and voice concerns about systems that exacerbate inequality."[38] No one individual, or manager, can resolve these risks. An agile manager in a volatile world does, however, have some role in addressing any number of internal risks for an organization. Internal risks are microeconomic in nature and deal with compliance, operational, financial, and reputational issues, among others. These internal risks threaten most organizations in a given year leaving managers learning how to navigate their response. The oft quoted "putting out fires" refers to figuring out how to respond to one micro crisis after another. Just how important are internal risks compared to external risks according to exec-utives? *The Executive Perspectives on Top Risks for 2020* report found "six of the top 10 risks reflect operational concerns, suggesting respondents con-tinue to be focused on operational issues to a greater extent than strategic or macroeconomic issues."[39] Agile managers in a volatile world, however, need to address a third category of risks focused on personal growth since "the important question to ask on the job is not, 'what am I getting?' but instead, 'what am I becoming?'"[40]

Personal growth risks include a wide spectrum of threats including the risk of conventional thinking, the risk of lacking a decision-making

---

[38] *The Global Risks Report 2020*, World Economic Forum, published January 15, 2020. https://weforum.org/reports/the-global-risks-report-2020

[39] "Executive Perspectives on Top Risks for 2020." Protiviti and North Carolina State University's Enterprise Risk Management Initiative. https://protiviti.com/CA-en/insights/protiviti-top-risks-survey

[40] Rohn, J. 2017. "Why Personal Development is Critical to Success." February 15, 2017, Jim Rohn blog. https://jimrohn.com/personal-development-critical-success/

process, and the risk of being comfortable. The agile manager in a volatile world needs to periodically remember that "a lack of self-awareness can leave executives in the dark about their impact on the business and the people who make it run."[41] American entrepreneur, author, and motivational speaker Jim Rohn understood the value of personal growth. His mentor Earl Shoaff once said to him, "If you want to be wealthy and happy, learn to work harder on yourself than you do on your job."[42] Shoaff's statement woke Rohn up and he continuously worked hard at his personal growth, describing it as "the most challenging assignment of all that lasted a lifetime."[43] Rohn's story illustrates how professional development is directly linked to personal growth. If an agile manager wants to grow professionally, they will have to grow personally.

In today's volatile world, "boards of directors and executive management teams cannot afford to manage risks casually on a reactive basis, especially considering the rapid pace of disruptive innovation and technological developments in an ever-advancing digital world."[44] To be an agile manager in a volatile world, one needs to couple a proactive approach with a high degree of self-awareness. "Accomplished leaders understand that self-awareness brings a sense of certainty in tough decision-making situations. This self-awareness enables them to make quicker and more efficient assessments in tough moments."[45] "A survey of 75 members of the Stanford Graduate School of Business Advisory Council rated

---

[41] Kiger, D. 2018. "Self-Awareness is Essential in Business Leadership." May 11, 2018, https://business2community.com/leadership/self-awareness-is-essential-in-business-leadership-02057971

[42] Rohn, J. 2017. "Why Personal Development is Critical to Success." February 15, 2017, Jim Rohn blog. https://jimrohn.com/personal-development-critical-success/

[43] Rohn, J. 2017. "Why Personal Development is Critical to Success." February 15, 2017, Jim Rohn blog. https://jimrohn.com/personal-development-critical-success/

[44] "Executive Perspectives on Top Risks for 2020." Protiviti and North Carolina State University's Enterprise Risk Management Initiative. https://protiviti.com/CA-en/insights/protiviti-top-risks-survey

[45] Kiger, D. "Self-Awareness is essential in business leadership," May 11, 2018, https://business2community.com/leadership/self-awareness-is-essential-in-business-leadership-02057971

self-awareness as the most important capability for leaders to develop. Executives need to know where their natural inclinations lie in order to boost them or compensate for them."[46] This dedication to develop or enhance one's national inclinations starts with a mindset that is open to new perspectives and is fully aware of the risk of conventional thinking.

Conventional thinking prevents the agile manager from considering new perspectives, engages one in blind thinking, and limits an ability to process new ideas. Since "limited perspectives lead to limited thinking," the agile manager who demonstrates a commitment to thinking differently remains open to the views of others and therefore can expand their perspectives to be more universally inclusive.[47] Highly creative people who think differently have figured out that failure is a learning experience and, as such, is a necessary and expected part of future success. As Jeff Dyer and Hal Gregersen concluded, from their study of over 5,000 entrepreneurs and executives, almost anyone who consistently makes the effort to think different can do so. Recognize that thinking differently is a tool available to any agile manager looking to combat the risk of conventional thinking. For example, individuals labeled as innovators of new businesses, products, and processes spend almost 50 percent more time trying to think different compared to noninnovators.[48]

But do recognize that thinking differently is hard work and that is why so few people, managers especially, choose to rely on conventional thinking and the path of least resistance. In April 1928 a journal called *The Forum* published an interview with Henry Ford who commented on the apparent increase in the complexity and rapidity of life. Ford was skeptical about whether there had been a commensurate increase in thought. According to Ford, "But there is a question in my mind whether, with all

---

[46] Toegel, g., and J.L. Barsoux. 2012. "How to Become a Better Leader." *MIT Sloan Management Review*, March 20, 2012. https://sloanreview.mit.edu/article/how-to-become-a-better-leader/

[47] Davis, T. 2019. "What is Self-Awareness, and How Do You Get It?" *Psychology Today*, March 11, 2019. https://psychologytoday.com/us/blog/click-here-happiness/201903/what-is-self-awareness-and-how-do-you-get-it

[48] Swallow, E. 2012. "Can Innovative Thinking Be Learned?" *Forbes*, April 19, 2012. https://forbes.com/sites/ericaswallow/2012/04/19/innovators-dna-hal-gregersen-interview/#47aaea054578

this speeding up of our everyday activities, there is any more real thinking. Thinking is the hardest work there is, which is the probable reason why so few engage in it."[49] Recent research continues to confirm Ford's observation from almost a century ago in that "people often refuse to relinquish their deep-seated beliefs even when presented with overwhelming evidence to contradict those beliefs."[50] One such person who let go of deep-seated beliefs and engaged in unconventional thinking was Sam Zell.

Businessman Sam Zell understood the value of unconventional thinking and holds investments in commercial real estate, energy, and other industries. Zell maintains substantial interests in, and is the chairman of, several public companies listed on the New York Stock Exchange and is chairman of Equity Group Investments (EGI), the private investment firm he founded in 1969. As Zell recalled in a *Forbes* interview, there were many times in his life when he would have liked to follow conventional thinking but instead followed his gut. But going against the herd can be really lonely. Zell told the story of a time in 1991 when he was standing in the lobby of a bank and wondered why no one else was interested in buying the building. His unconventional way of thinking saw the purchase as an incredible opportunity. "By 1994 all those people were there in line, but the bulk of the opportunity had passed. Upon review of *The Forbes 400* list and take off everybody who inherited money, what's left are people who went right when everyone else went left. Conventional wisdom leads to mediocrity."[51] In today's volatile world, the agile manager has no time to be mediocre and needs to rely upon a strong decision-making process.

To be an effective manager in today's VUCA global marketplace, decision-making skills are crucial. As author Caitlin McCormack wrote, "although your skills as an individual helped you land this job, your effectiveness as a decision-maker is what will help you succeed in this role and

---

[49] 1928 April, *The Forum*, Volume 79, Number 4. "My Philosophy of Industry" by Henry Ford. Interview conducted by Fay Leone Faurote, p. 481. The Forum Publishing Company, New York.

[50] Klapper, B. 2013. "Free Yourself from Conventional Thinking." *Harvard Business Review*, May 8, 2013. https://hbr.org/2013/05/free-yourself-from-conventiona

[51] Sam Zell interview in *Forbes*, September 28, 2017. https://pressreader.com/usa/forbes/20170928/282295320340883

any other future roles, e.g. in project management."[52] Lacking a decision-making process, however, often leads one to second guess themselves, needing to involve the entire team before committing or failing to trust their instinct. With no clear decision-making process, a manager runs the risk of losing the respect of employees, missing deadlines, and jeopardizing the outcomes of important projects. Since so few people mitigate the risk of conventional thinking by thinking differently, it's no surprise most managers lack a decision-making process and fail to keep track of the outcomes of their decisions. "As a result, most organizations are not very good at decision making."[53] In one study of 500 managers and executives researchers found that 98 percent fail to apply best practices when making decisions.[54] Agile managers can ill afford to continue to ignore the risk of lacking a decision-making process. Sustainability in today's hypercompetitive world is dependent upon the manager maintaining the necessary degree of self-awareness in order to recognize, assess, and improve their decision-making process. As David Brooks wrote in a *New York Times* editorial, "It's becoming incredibly important to learn to decide well, to develop the techniques of self-distancing to counteract the flaws in our own mental machinery."[55]

One person who developed an efficient decision-making model was former U.S. president Dwight D. Eisenhower. In a 1954 speech to the Second Assembly of the World Council of Churches Eisenhower said: "I have two kinds of problems: the urgent and the important. The urgent

---

[52] McCormack, C. 2018. "7 Decision Making Tips for New Managers." *Monday Blog*, September 18, 2018. https://monday.com/blog/7-decision-making-tips-for-new-managers/

[53] Larson, E. 2017. "Don't Fail at Decision Making Like 98% of Managers Do." *Forbes*, May 18, 2017. https://forbes.com/sites/eriklarson/2017/05/18/research-reveals-7-steps-to-better-faster-decision-making-for-your-business-team/#120e4b9e40ad

[54] Larson, E. 2017. "Don't Fail at Decision Making like 98% of Managers Do." *Forbes*, May 18, 2017. https://forbes.com/sites/eriklarson/2017/05/18/research-reveals-7-steps-to-better-faster-decision-making-for-your-business-team/#120e4b9e40ad

[55] Brooks, D. 2016. "The Choice Explosion." *The New York Times*, May 3, 2016. https://nytimes.com/2016/05/03/opinion/the-choice-explosion.html

are not important, and the important are never urgent." Often referred to as the "Eisenhower principle" on organizing workload and priorities, this decision-making process involves a 2 × 2 grid consisting of four categories:

- Urgent and important (tasks to do immediately)—*do it*
- Important, but not urgent (tasks to schedule later)—*defer it*
- Urgent, but not important (tasks to delegate to someone else)—*delegate it*
- Neither urgent nor important (tasks to eliminate)—*delete it.*

Also known as the 4D approach to decision making—do it, defer it, delegate it, or delete it—Eisenhower's approach can help the agile manager understand that great time management means being effective as well as efficient. The agile manager needs to prioritize spending time on those tasks that fall into the important and urgent categories. Understanding the distinction between issues, tasks, and problems empowers the manager to be much more agile and respond appropriately. Without a decision-making process or model, it is virtually impossible for the manager to distinguish between what is important and/or urgent so therefore every single issue is both important and urgent; a woefully inefficient and ineffective way to manage. "When we know which activities are important and which are urgent, we can overcome the natural tendency to focus on unimportant urgent activities, so that we can clear enough time to do what's essential for our success. This is the way we move from 'firefighting' into a position where we can grow our businesses and our careers."[56] But such growth comes at the risk of being comfortable.

For the agile manager looking to achieve and sustain growth today, they will need to identify how often they resort to being comfortable. There is seldom any growth when one is in a state of comfortableness. Personal growth and professional development are linked to one's self-awareness when coupled with a willingness to travel outside of one's comfort zone. Often referred to as psychological or cognitive

---

[56] "Eisenhower's Urgent/Important Principle." *Blog post*, https://mindtools.com/pages/article/newHTE_91.htm

disequilibrium, by definition being uncomfortable refers to, an unset-
tling stimulus or experience that disrupts one's previously established
belief structure. Such a trait is often found in the backstories of successful people. Disequilibrium can be produced by almost any stimulus that
agitates one's current way of understanding and being. Today's volatile
global economy has no shortage of opportunities that agitates a manager's current way of conducting business. According to Nevitt Sanford,
the experience of psychological and cognitive disequilibrium produces
feelings of internal dissonance that manifests itself as uncertainty, and
sometimes as conflict and even threat. "But it is the experience of such
dissonance that opens up the possibility for learning and growth because
it nudges individuals into confronting and considering new ways of
understanding, thinking, and acting that help to unsettle the old and
integrate it with the new."[57]

As Alina Tugend observed, "being slightly uncomfortable, whether or
not by choice, can push us to achieve goals we never thought we could."[58]
Recognizing that individuals don't need to challenge themselves all the
time, Tugend concluded that although it is good to step out of our comfort zone, it is also good to go back in when necessary.[59] Agile managers
subscribe to a belief that hope and potential are around the corner. As
New York Times columnist David Brooks observed, "Almost every successful person begins with two beliefs: the future can be better than the
present, and I have the power to make it so."[60] Even if they have no idea
how they are going to make it happen, they start and find a way to move

---

[57] Dalton, J., and P. Crosby. 2008. "Challenging College Students to Learn
in Campus Cultures of Comfort, Convenience and Complacency." *Journal of
College and Character* 9, no. 3, DOI: 10.2202/1940-1639.1112 To link to this
article: https://doi.org/10.2202/1940-163

[58] Tugend, A. 2011. "Tiptoeing Out of One's Comfort Zone (and of Course, Back
in)." *The New York Times*, February 11, 2011. https://nytimes.com/2011/02/12/
your-money/12shortcuts.html

[59] Tugend, A. 2011. "Tiptoeing Out of One's Comfort Zone (and of Course, Back
in)," *The New York Times*, February 11, 2011. https://nytimes.com/2011/02/12/
your-money/12shortcuts.html

[60] Brooks, D. 2008. "Lost in the Crowd," *The New York Times*, December 15,
2008. https://nytimes.com/2008/12/16/opinion/16brooks.html

forward one step at a time. Google cofounder Larry Page talked about this when he gave a speech describing how he had a "healthy disregard for the impossible and wrote down the things I thought were impossible but wanted to accomplish anyway. We were close to not starting Google. Do not be afraid of failure. Instead, have the goal to fail a lot and eventually you will succeed. Take a little more risk in life and if you do it often enough it will pay off."[61] Page had a healthy disregard for the impossible and worked through being uncomfortable.

Identifying the personal growth issues related to the risk of conventional thinking, the risk of lacking a decision-making process, and the risk of being comfortable are critical for anyone looking to be an agile manager in a volatile world. As Douglas A. Ready discovered in his team's research into the mindsets of executives on how to succeed in a volatile economy "adopting new mindsets and behaviors" as well as the importance of finding approaches that would reinforce and embed these mindsets and behaviors as the new hallmarks of leadership.[62] "Organizations looking to best the competition must embrace the need to adapt by encouraging new ideas brought about by as many non-traditional interactions as possible."[63] "Their self-knowledge clears space so they can cut through the confusion, making their commitment to decisions more fluid. Successful leaders use observation and learning to become experts at knowing patterns of business and behavior, enabling them to take more risk with less loss."[64] One of the most powerful tools available to the agile manager willing to observe and learn is asking questions (Principle #3).

---

[61] Page, L. "On How To Achieve Success." *Video Presentation Located* at https://goalcast.com/2017/01/15/larry-page-on-how-to-achieve-success/

[62] Ready, D.A. 2019. "Leadership Mindsets for the New Economy." *MIT Sloan Management Review,* November 6, 2019. https://sloanreview.mit.edu/article/leadership-mindsets-for-the-new-economy/

[63] Klapper, B. 2013. "Free Yourself From Conventional Thinking." *Harvard Business Review,* May 8, 2013. https://hbr.org/2013/05/free-yourself-from-conventiona

[64] Kiger, D. 2018. "Self-Awareness is Essential in Business Leadership." May 11, 2018, https://business2community.com/leadership/self-awareness-is-essential-in-business-leadership-02057971

Principle #3: Ask Questions

Asking questions is the third principle of the agile manager looking to improve their function as a curator in today's volatile world. Taking the time to reflect and ask big picture questions, engaging in double-loop learning opportunities, and encouraging employees to ask questions can help increase a manager's agility in a volatile world. Once the agile manager understands the landscape (Principle #1) and identifies the risks (Principle #2), they can ask questions and allow employees to do the same (Principle #3). For some agile managers, it may be uncomfortable to ask strategic questions and engage employees in a conversation about matters both small and large relative to the organization's sustainability. To avoid the difficult conversations, however, would jeopardize the function of the manager as curator. This principle of asking questions and remaining open to discussing answers demonstrates self-awareness and a willingness to learn. "Plus, asking questions models a solid, transparent approach to problem-solving and decision-making that benefits everyone in an organization. But perhaps most importantly, it models that it is okay not to know everything, which encourages everyone that it's okay to be constantly learning." [65] The agile manager should be aware of their own strengths and weaknesses. "Honest self-evaluation will help supervisors get the most out of themselves and the team they lead."[66] Asking critical strategic questions is the third principle within the function of the manager as curator.

As previously discussed, managers often find themselves overwhelmed and constantly "putting out fires." The agile manager operating in a volatile world will indeed be quite busy. But being busy all the time is counterproductive and means they lack the skill to prioritize the time required to think and reflect. Managers need to understand the fundamental belief that "thinking is in fact quite an important activity when it

---

[65] Toegel, G., and J.L. Barsoux. 2012. "How to Become a Better Leader." *MIT Sloan Management Review* March 20, 2012. https://sloanreview.mit.edu/article/how-to-become-a-better-leader/

[66] Gottsman, D. 2017. "8 Critical Questions for Managers to Ask Themselves." *Inc. Magazine*, January 4, 2017. https://inc.com/diane-gottsman/8-critical-questions-for-managers-to-ask-themselves.html

comes to assessing and developing a strategy."[67] To help the agile manager you here are just a few examples of critical strategic questions that the organization needs to be thinking about if it hopes to remain relevant, vibrant, and vital.

- Is the organization's product or service still relevant?
- Why are we doing what we are doing?
- What strategic imperatives must be accomplished for the organization to achieve both short-term and long-term sustainability?
- What part of the organization is likely to be impacted by innovative and disruptive technologies in the future?
- Where should the organization first implement a more agile approach to business?

There are dozens of other questions throughout this publication for the agile manager operating in a volatile world. Questions appear at the end of each chapter and then the entire list can be located in Appendix III. Managers looking to increase their organizations' agility will need to both acknowledge and reject the business situation they inherited and find substantial periods of careful, undisturbed reflection, and consideration. Doing so will allow managers to make "complex decisions under uncertainty, with substantive, long-term consequences. Managing is not just about doing things it is also about thinking. Make time for it."[68] Nick Mehta, CEO of Gainsight, a customer success software company with more than 600 employees, emphasized the need for managers to think when he wrote "if you're a manager there's a question you need to ask yourself. It's fundamentally a question about what it means to lead. The question is 'Are you giving your team everything they need

---

[67] Vermeulen, F. 2015. "5 Strategy Questions Every Leader Should Make Time For." *Harvard Business Review*, September 3, 2015. https://hbr.org/2015/09/5-strategy-questions-every-leader-should-make-time-for

[68] Vermeulen, F. 2015. "5 Strategy Questions Every Leader Should Make Time For." *Harvard Business Review*, September 3, 2015. https://hbr.org/2015/09/5-strategy-questions-every-leader-should-make-time-for

to succeed?'"[69] Why is this so important to Mehta? Simply because "the role of a leader isn't to tell people what to do, it's to give them the resources they need to thrive."[70] And one exercise agile managers can use to process the answer to this question, as well as other employees might have, is known as double-loop learning.

The valuable cognitive approach known as double-loop learning was developed by Harvard Business School professor Chris Argyris in 1970s and offers managers a valuable tool use to solve problems. Double-loop learning is a process that allows individuals to ask the critical question, "why are we doing this?" in order to challenge underlying assumptions, norms, and objectives.[71] Double-loop learning provides a more sophisticated, internal, and relevant decision-making exercise compared to single-loop learning. Relying on a single-loop learning process involves three characteristics: (1) it is an insular mental process, (2) people consider possible external or technical reasons for obstacles, and (3) current policies or objectives continue unchallenged. Managers who develop the habit of engaging in single-loop learning allow a company to hide its problems, lead to rigidity, deterioration, and ultimately irrelevance. Former president of the Strategic Management Society, Henry Mitzberg, wrote "Every manager has a mental model of the world in which he or she acts based on experience and knowledge. When a manager must make a decision, he or she thinks of behavior alternatives within their mental model."[72] This is single-loop learning.

---

[69] Mehta, N. 2019. "An Experienced CEO Says there's One Question All Managers Should Ask Themselves Every Day—Especially When Things Go Wrong." *Business Insider,* May 7, 2019. https://businessinsider.com/nick-mehta-one-question-all-managers-should-ask-themselves-2019-5

[70] Mehta, N. 2019. "An Experienced CEO says there's One Question All Managers should Ask Themselves Every Day—Especially When Things Go Wrong." *Business Insider,* May 7, 2019. https://businessinsider.com/nick-mehta-one-question-all-managers-should-ask-themselves-2019-5

[71] Argyris, C. September 1977. "Double Loop Learning in Organizations," *Harvard Business Review,* https://hbr.org/1977/09/double-loop-learning-in-organizations

[72] Mintzberg, H. 1994. *Rise and Fall of Strategic Planning.* https://tinyurl.com/v7jzzzf

For example, consider a thermostat that can be programmed to turn on or off when the room temperature reaches a certain point. All the thermostat can do is go up or down based on its programming: single-loop learning. It can never ask itself (a) why am I programmed to go off or on at a certain point, (b) is the temperature set at a reasonable level, or (c) is there a better way to create a more comfortable room setting? The agile manager in a volatile world can ill afford to not ask the question, "Why are we doing what we are doing?" These questions represent a far more effective cognitive approach that involves questioning every aspect of the approach, methodology, biases, and deeply held assumptions related to a specific situation; also known as double-loop learning.

This approach also relies on a heightened level of self-awareness, which many people are hesitant to pursue. This more psychologically nuanced self-examination requires that the agile manager honestly challenge their beliefs and summon the courage to act on that information. Such action may lead to fresh ways of thinking about the organization's goals, strategic imperatives to accomplish them, and the managerial approaches to move forward. Using double-loop learning allows the agile manager to both redesign the goal and the underlying thinking being used to achieve it. As researcher Sharon Cartwright noted, "the results of successful double-loop learning and the process of dialogue that accompanies it can, however, be well worth the challenge."[73] Experimentation with new designs and new actions, with an emphasis on providing opportunities for people to rethink why they are doing what they are doing, are all opportunities for the agile manager to encourage people to ask questions.

Since "80% of senior leaders believe good employee engagement is a critical part of achieving business objectives," then the agile manager needs to encourage people to ask questions.[74] Perhaps nowhere is this

---

[73] Cartwright, S. 2002. "Double-Loop Learning: A Concept and Process for Leadership Educators," *Journal of Leadership Education* 1, no. 1, https://journalofleadershiped.org/jole_articles/double-loop-learning-a-concept-and-process-for-leadership-educators/

[74] Wiles, J. 2018. "9 Questions that Should be in Every Employee Engagement Survey." *Gartner*, November 19, 2018. https://gartner.com/smarterwithgartner/the-9-questions-that-should-be-in-every-employee-engagement-survey/

more important than in meetings. Unfortunately, the amount of time spent in meetings continues to increase and often has a negative impact on the work culture and discourages people to ask questions. Leslie A. Perlow and her colleagues surveyed 182 senior managers across a range of industries and their research found:

- 65 percent said meetings keep them from completing their own work.
- 71 percent said meetings are unproductive and inefficient.
- 64 percent said meetings come at the expense of deep thinking.
- 62 percent said meetings miss opportunities to bring the team closer together.[75]

The agile manager in a volatile world certainly wants to maximize each employee's contribution. With research results like these, it is obvious that meetings run counter to helping each person perform their best. Encouraging people to ask questions involves finding better ways for the manager to communicate with team members through one on one conversation, informal discussions over lunch, or simply taking a walk outside and discussing the topic of the day. If a meeting is absolutely necessary, then the manager needs to create an environment conducive of open communication. "The quest for better meetings ultimately lies in leading with mutual respectful, inclusivity, and establishing a space that is safe enough for people to speak their minds."[76]

One of the most common and effective strategies agile managers can use in a volatile world is a variation on the approach known as management by walking around (MBWA). First coined in their 1982 *In Search of Excellence: Lessons from America's Best Run Companies*, Tom Peters and

[75] Perlow, L.A., C.N. Hadley, and E. Eun, 2017. "Stop the Meeting Madness." *Harvard Business Review*, July–August 2017. https://hbr.org/2017/07/stop-the-meeting-madness

[76] Axtell, P. 2019. "Make your Meetings a Safe Space for Honest Conversation." *Harvard Business Review*, April 11, 2019. https://hbr.org/2019/04/make-your-meetings-a-safe-space-for-honest-conversation

Robert H. Waterman defined the concept as the practice of managers randomly strolling through their company locations, stopping to chat or observe, all in an unplanned fashion.[77] This effective communication strategy encourages people to ask questions and engage in an open conversation about key issues. Instead of the typical "what are you working on?" questions managers ask during the "walk around," David Kalt identified the following four effective questions managers should consider asking employees:

- What has been (or will be) your biggest win this week?
- What challenges are you facing?
- How do you think our competitors would respond to this?
- What were some great contributions made by other team members recently?[78]

"These queries might not feel natural at first, but stepping outside of your normal line of questioning and thinking critically and creatively about the questions you ask during one-on-ones, status updates, and team meetings is an instant way to learn more about your employees and their work."[79] In addition to physically walking around, the agile manager should also consider checking in with employees via phone calls and video conference calls to engage those working virtually or in another location. While the aforementioned four questions are good to start with, remember there are plenty of questions to ask. According to Hal Gregersen, the best questions

---

[77] Belyh, A. 2017. "Management by Walking Around (MBWA)—The Essential Guide." March 11, 2017. https://cleverism.com/management-by-walking-around-mbwa/

[78] Kalt, D. 2018. "Four Effective Questions to Ask Your Staff During Casual Conversations." *The Wall Street Journal,* June 18, 2018. https://blogs.wsj.com/experts/2018/06/18/four-effective-questions-to-ask-your-staff-during-casual-conversations/

[79] Kalt, D. 2018. "Four Effective Questions to Ask your Staff During Casual Conversations." *The Wall Street Journal,* June 18, 2018. https://blogs.wsj.com/experts/2018/06/18/four-effective-questions-to-ask-your-staff-during-casual-conversations/

"knock down barriers to creative thinking and channel energy down new, more productive pathways and contains five traits:

- It *reframes* the problem.
- It *intrigues* the imagination.
- It *invites* others' thinking.
- It *opens up space* for different answers.
- And it's *nonaggressive*—not posed to embarrass, humiliate or assert power over the other party.

One of the best examples of a question that includes all five attributes is "If you were in my shoes, what would you be doing differently than what you see us doing today?"[80] The agile manager in a volatile world needs to possess both the confidence and self-awareness to not only ask this question but also engage in a conversation with the employee regarding their answer. This engagement opens the door for future communications and illustrates to the employee that the manager takes the time to ask relevant questions, engage in a conversation, and allows room for employees to ask questions.

Taking the time to reflect and ask big picture questions, engaging in double-loop learning opportunities, and encouraging employees to ask questions can help increase a manager's agility in a volatile world. Asking good questions is a standard operating procedure and good practice for managers. "Doing so in a spirit of honest information gathering and collaboration cultivates an environment where staff feel comfortable discussing issues that affect both their performance and that of the team. That, in turn, creates a foundation for deepening levels of trust, increasing morale and innovation, and enhancing productivity."[81] Understanding the landscape (Principle #1),

---

[80] Gregersen, H. 2019. "The Secret to Asking Better Questions." *The Wall Street Journal,* May 9, 2019. https://wsj.com/articles/to-be-a-better-leader-ask-better-questions-11557426294

[81] Cheverie, J. 2017. "Why Asking Good Questions can Help you be a Better Leader." *The Professional Development Commons,* February 13, 2017. https://er.educause.edu/blogs/2017/2/why-asking-good-questions-can-help-you-be-a-better-leader

identifying risks (Principle #2), and asking questions (Principle #3) can help the agile manager function as a curator. Curating this knowledge helps build the foundation for the second function of an agile manager—architect— one who designs the mission, vision, and values for an organization looking to achieve and sustain growth in a volatile world.

Questions

Principle #1: Understand the Landscape

- How often do you study the macro trends in your industry?
- How do your employees respond when you discuss VUCA trends?
- What are you doing to help them better understand VUCA trends?
- When you do study them how do you relay that information?
- Do you send reports, information, and other items to your team in the hopes they read and understand the need to change?
- How has today's VUCA environment impacted your organization and what changes have you made/do you still need to make, to achieve and sustain growth?
- Do you have a task force devoted to studying the trends and suggesting changes?
- Are you comfortable with having others recommend agile moves?
- Are you practicing the time-honored tradition of micromanagement and telling people what to do and how to do it when it comes to change management?
- How often are you challenging your people to grow and providing them the support to do so?
- How has hyperconnectedness changed your business?
- How comfortable are you with change, especially constant and intense change?
- How well do you manage uncertainty and being able to move forward without knowing?

- How do you respond to complex situations involving multiple factors?
- How often do you thrive in ambiguity?

Principle #2: Identify Risks

- How often do you think about the various types of risks associated with being a manager?
- How often do you identify personal growth risks that could impact being an agile manager?
- What prevents you from thinking differently?
- How often do you catch yourself engaging in conventional thinking?
- What is your decision-making process?
- How often do you look to improve your decision-making process?
- What prevents you from improving your decision-making process?
- Have you noticed the decision-making process of others?
- How often do you travel outside of your comfort zone?
- How comfortable are you being uncomfortable?

Principle #3: Ask Questions

- How often do you think about the critical questions related to the future of your organization?
- How often do you discuss the need to change to remain relevant?
- Does everyone on your team know why they are doing what they are doing? How do you know?
- How often do you walk around and engage in open conversations with employees?
- For those team members working virtually, how often do you check in on them?
- Have you assessed the types of questions you ask employees?

- What attributes do your questions have?
- How have you worked to improve your listening skills lately?
- Now that you have covered the three principles related to the agile manager as a curator, spend time reflecting on your ability to curate information. How has your ability to function as a curator improve?

CHAPTER 4

Architect

Introduction to Function #2: Architect

The second function of an agile manager is that of an architect designing the mission, vision, and values on an organization in a volatile world. These attributes of an organization are synonymous with the three architectural concerns of foundation, façade, and design of a building. Just as the three concerns for the architect are interrelated, so too are the three attributes for an agile manager. The mission (foundation), vision (façade), and values (design) are three separate, yet interrelated components of a dynamic entity. The foundation needs to be strong enough to support the design that requires a level of innovation to be attractive using a façade that is energy efficient and compliments the design. Organizations operating in a VUCA environment must rely upon a strong mission, a clear vision, and the right set of values to achieve and sustain growth. Thus, it is imperative that the agile manager work on each attribute separately while understanding the contribution of each one to the other. "As an architect you design for the present," English architect Norman Foster wrote, "with an awareness of the past, for a future which is essentially unknown."[1] Such an observation could serve as a guiding light for the agile manager in a volatile world.

Leveraging the information gathered as a curator (function #1), the agile manager can create or update an organization's mission to remain relevant (Principle #4). As retired U.S. Army general Eric Ken Shinseki said: "If you dislike change, you're going to dislike irrelevance even more."[2] Managers looking to develop their agility should heed Shinseki's

---

[1] TED Talk: Norman Foster on Green Architecture, DLD 2007 Conference, https://archdaily.com/777366/ted-talk-norman-foster-on-green-architecture
[2] Shinseki, E. Wikipedia, https://en.wikiquote.org/wiki/Eric_Shinseki

words closely. Technological disruptions continue to alter the very fabric of life and work so a review of an organization's mission statement is only prudent for the agile manager. Upon review of the mission, the agile manager can work toward designing the vision of an organization (Principle #5). Designing a vision will allow the agile manager to maintain an organization's focus while navigating the chaos of a volatile world. Once the mission is reviewed and updated if necessary and the vision designed, an agile manager can cultivate the values of an organization's culture (Principle #6). The values drive the expectations, behaviors, and attitudes of employees and help the organization maintain consistency of work across departments and functional areas.

Principle #4: Update the Mission

This history of business is littered with examples of companies that leverage agility to develop new-growth businesses by updating the original mission statement or traditional core business model. A mission statement is a concise explanation of the organization's reason for existence and describes the organization's purpose and overall intention. Propelling companies to achieve and sustain growth in turbulent times often involves a new approach to business, thinking differently, and remaining open to sustainability measures.[3] In his article "18 Mistakes That Kill Startups," venture capitalist Paul Graham highlighted the need to be agile and wrote: "Don't get too attached to your original plan, because it's probably wrong. Most successful startups end up doing something different than they originally intended—often so different that it doesn't even seem like the same company."[4] Development as an agile manager will depend upon an ability "to be prepared to see the better idea when

---

[3] Anthony, S.D., A. Trotter, and E.I. Schwartz. 2019. "The Top 20 Business Transformations of the Last Decade." September 24, 2019, *Harvard Business Review*, https://hbr.org/2019/09/the-top-20-business-transformations-of-the-last-decade

[4] Paul Graham, "The 18 Mistakes that Kill Startups," October 2006. www.paulgraham.com/startupmistakes.html

it arrives. And the hardest part of that is often discarding your old idea."[5] Fortunately, as a manager looking to develop agility in today's volatile world, history provides ample examples of organizations who remained agile to update their mission statement or revise the business model in order to achieve and sustain growth. Author's note: Each company listed as follows has a long history that deserve far more than the limited space provided here. The following time periods are utilized for summary purposes. Refer to the references for additional information. The following list is in alphabetical order.

Abercrombie & Fitch

- *Original mission*: Over 125 years ago, David T. Abercrombie founded the New York City based company in 1892 as an outfitter for the elite outdoorsman. Eight years later, in 1900, devoted customer and real-estate developer Ezra Fitch bought a significant interest in the business. In 1904, it was incorporated and renamed "Abercrombie & Fitch Co." For six decades, the company sustained itself on providing outdoorsman apparel for the likes of Ernest Hemingway, Teddy Roosevelt, and other elites. By the 1970s, however, the business was struggling with lower priced competition while trying to maintain its position as a high-end retailer.[6]
- *Second business model*: In 1976, Abercrombie & Fitch filed for Chapter 11 bankruptcy and eventually shuttered its flagship store at Madison Avenue and East 45th Street the following year. Jake Oshman, owner of the Houston-based chain Oshman's Sporting Goods, bought Abercrombie & Fitch's mailing list

---

[5] Graham, P. 2006. "The 18 mistakes that kill startups," October 2006. www.paulgraham.com/startupmistakes.html

[6] Schlossberg, M. 2016. "The Bizarre History of Abercrombie & Fitch—and how the Retailer is Transforming Yet Again." *Business Insider*, January 12, 2016. https://businessinsider.com/abercrombie-fitch-crazy-history-2011-4

for $1.5 million and relaunched the company as a mail-order retailer specializing in hunting wear and novelty items.[7]

- *Third business model*: In 1988, Oshman sold the company name and operations to The Limited, a clothing-chain operator based in Columbus, Ohio. It gradually shifted its focus to young adults, first as a subsidiary of Limited Brands and then as a separate, publicly traded company and grew to become one of the largest apparel firms in the United States. As of December 2019, total global sales exceeded $3.9 billion.[8]

Amazon

- *Original mission*: In 1994 Jeff Bezos and his wife MacKenzie open an online bookstore in Seattle because of the city's reputation as a tech hub. During 1997 and 1998 Amazon went public, added music and videos, and launched global operations in the United Kingdom and Germany. By 2000 the company expanded its online bookstore to include consumer electronics, home-improvement items, software, games, and toys in addition to other items.

---

[7] Schlossberg, M. 2016. "The Bizarre History of Abercrombie & Fitch—and How the Retailer is Transforming Yet Again." *Business Insider*, January 12, 2016. https://businessinsider.com/abercrombie-fitch-crazy-history-2011-4. Additional resources include: Wu, J. 2019. "Here's How Abercrombie & Fitch Ditched its Past to Try to Bring Back Customers." *CNBC*, October 16, 2019. https://tinyurl.com/yy4ega8g; Abercrombie & Fitch Company History website located at https://corporate.abercrombie.com/our-company/about-us/company-history; Lamare, A. 2018. "The History of Abercrombie & Fitch, A Brand Searching for a New Identity." https://media.thinknum.com/articles/abercrombie-and-fitch-hollister-history-relevancy-crisis/; and Park, G. 2018. "Abercrombie & Fitch: Grappling with Heritage." September 10, 2018. https://grailed.com/drycleanonly/abercrombie-fitch-history
[8] "Analysts Expect Over 2019 Rising Revenue Abercrombie & Fitch, Relatively High Dividend" May 29, 2019. https://tinyurl.com/srzj2t3

- *First update to mission*: In 2002, the corporation started Amazon Web Services (AWS), which provided data on Web site popularity, Internet traffic patterns, and other statistics for marketers and developers. This update to its original mission of being an online bookstore allowed the company to generate income by licensing its platform to other e-commerce sites, like Borders.com and Target.com.
- *Second update to mission*: In 2006 Amazon launched Prime Video, an American Internet video on-demand service offering television shows and films for rent or purchase and Prime Video, a selection of Amazon Studios original content and licensed acquisitions included in the Amazon's Prime subscription.
- *Third update to mission*: In 2007, Amazon launched its Kindle, an e-reader device enabling users to browse, buy, download, and read e-books, newspapers, magazines, and other digital media via wireless networking to the Kindle Store.
- *Fourth update to mission*: In 2017 Amazon purchased Whole Foods for $13.7 billion and increased its position in the highly competitive grocery delivery business.[9]

In his 1997 Annual Report Letter to Shareholders, Bezos proclaimed his relentless focus to obsess over customers. To do that, he has relied upon bold rather than timid decisions.[10] This obsession and bold decision-making process has allowed Amazon to update its mission time and again. By continually updating its mission, Amazon became a leader in global commerce, changed the way people consume, and reinvented the very notion of convenience.

---

[9] DePillis, L., and I. Sherman. 2018. "Amazon's extraordinary 25-year evolution," CNN Business. https://cnn.com/interactive/2018/10/business/amazon-history-timeline/index.html

[10] Letter located at https://tinyurl.com/ycw5dc9e.

Nintendo

- *Original mission*: Over 130 years ago, Fusajiro Yamauchi founded Nintendo in September 1889. Its original mission called for the production of handmade *hanafuda* playing cards. *Hanafuda* playing cards, also known as flower cards, are used to play a number of games. The company continued on its original mission for six decades.[11] By 1950, over hundred people worked at Nintendo and the founder's 22-year-old great-grandson was placed in charge of continuing the original mission. Times were changing, however, and he needed to demonstrate his agility if the company was to sustain forward momentum.
- *Second business model*: Once sales for the *hanafuda* playing cards decreased in the late 1950s, Nintendo engaged in scattershot investing and launched several small niche businesses in the early 1960s such as cab services and love hotels. These new ventures had little success, however, so the young president reinvented Nintendo.
- *Third business model*: Abandoning previous ventures in favor of toys in 1966, Nintendo's maintenance engineer Gunpei Yokoi helped usher in the company's third business model. Yokoi created the Ultra Hand, an extendable arm developed in his free time. His creativity was the catalyst that allowed Yokoi to graduate from maintenance to the product developer of the newly formed "Nintendo Games" department.[12] Yokoi's ability to find novel applications for technology others considered outdated was the source for his agility. Such an approach helped him launch the Game & Watch brand offering customers a series of handheld electronic games from 1980

---

[11] "History of Nintendo: Where did Nintendo come from?" https://bbc.co.uk/newsround/48606526

[12] Segarra, L.M. 2019. "As Game Boy Turns 30, It's Time to Recognize Its Inventor, Nintendo's Maintenance Man." *Fortune*, August 1, 2019. https://fortune.com/2019/08/01/nintendo-game-boy-release-date-inventor-gunpei-yokoi/

to 1991. The Game & Watch brand served as the precursor to Nintendo's most popular product Game Boy. Launched in 1989, one million units of Game Boy were sold in the United States within a few weeks. Over time, Game Boy and its successor, Game Boy Color, would go on to sell more than 110 million units worldwide.[13]

- *Update to third business model*: In 2017 Nintendo elevated its stake in the gaming market by launching the Nintendo Switch, a video game with the dual functionality of a home console and portable device. As of December 2019, the Nintendo Switch and Switch Lite has sold more than 52 million units worldwide. In February 2020, while video game sales continued to decline in the United States, Nintendo Switch hardware sales still surpassed its aging and outgoing competition. "Nintendo Switch was the best-selling hardware platform of February in both unit and dollar sales," NPD analyst Mat Piscatella said. "And [it] remains the best-selling hardware platform of the year."[14]

Individuals wishing to develop their agility to manage in a volatile world can learn a variety of lessons from these examples. First, recognize the historical track record of companies that achieved and sustained growth by updating their mission statements. There are many other organizations that had to reinvent themselves during the last few decades. Understanding this gives today's agile manager an entire set of reference points. Second, realize the value of launching innovative "outside the core" products and services. By going beyond the familiar markets and competencies on which the company has built its existing business, the agile manager can support "outside-the-core innovation projects targeting new customers

---

[13] An excellent summary of Nintendo's history is found in Epstein, D. 2019. *Range: Why Generalists Triumph in A Specialized World*. Riverhead Books, New York, Chapter 9.

[14] Grubb, J. 2020. "Nintendo Switch leads February 2020 Hardware Sales." *Venture Beat*, March 13, 2020. https://venturebeat.com/2020/03/13/nintendo-switch-leads-february-2020-hardware-sales/

or non-consumers in new markets to help drive growth."[15] Third, as with any strategic move, it is imperative that the agile manager understand the risks associated with outside-the-core thinking. Implementing such a strategic move requires one to understand "the risk of failure is influenced by false assumptions about the distribution channels, cost structure, unit margins, and velocity elements of the innovation, which are often carried over from the incumbent business model."[16] Fourth, any update to the mission or implementation of an outside-the-core strategy will take time and involve the support of various internal stakeholders. In short, updating the mission statement, reinventing the business model, or offering outside-the-core products and services are all tools in the armamentarium of the agile manager in a volatile world marked by constant change. Remember "companies thrive because they were willing to change with the shifting factors around their businesses."[17] Agile managers help drive such change.

On August 19, 2019, the Business Roundtable issued its "Statement on the Purpose of a Corporation." In one of the most significant developments in recent business history, this proclamation illustrated how companies are willing to change in today's volatile world. Signed by over 180 CEOs this "Statement" declared that serving shareholders can no longer be the main purpose of a corporation; rather, it needs to be about serving society, through innovation, commitment to a healthy environment and economic opportunity for all. According to the document, "Americans deserve an economy that allows each person to succeed through hard work and creativity and to lead a life of meaning and dignity."[18] This declaration

---

[15] Bertels, H.M. 2015. "Business Models Outside the Core: Lessons Learned from Success and Failure." *Research—Technology Management* 58, no. 2, https://tandfonline.com/doi/abs/10.5437/08956308X5802294#metrics-content
[16] Bertels, H.M. 2015. "Business Models Outside the Core: Lessons Learned from Success and Failure." *Research—Technology Management* 58, no. 2, https://tandfonline.com/doi/abs/10.5437/08956308X5802294#metrics-content
[17] Thomas, A. "5 Companies that Prove you Must Evolve to Thrive," *Inc.,* https://inc.com/andrew-thomas/5-companies-that-prove-you-must-evolve-to-thrive.html
[18] "Business ROUNDTABLE REDEFINES the purpose of a Corporation to Promote 'An Economy that Serves All Americans." August 19, 2019. https://tinyurl.com/v8w4e7u

is helping to shape the future of American commerce and illustrates the need to develop a vision (Principle #5).

Principle #5: Design a Vision

The fourth principle of updating the mission or business model compliments the fifth principle of designing a vision. The function of an architect allows the agile manager to understand how the mission and vision, while interrelated, are also different and complement one another. The vision, or vision statement, provides a source of inspiration for employees, customers, and management and paints an aspirational view of the future. Like mission statements, visions can change based on any number of internal and external factors. As an agile manager today, it is important to remember the observation of long-time University of Notre Dame president Theodore Hesburg who noted, "the very essence of leadership is that you have a vision. It's got to be a vision you articulate clearly and forcefully on every occasion. You can't blow an uncertain trumpet."[19] The agile manager can "blow a certain trumpet" by designing, articulating, and revising a vision that ensures the organizations vitality, relevance, and sustainability. The following vignettes illustrate vision development across different industries and serve as a reminder to today's manager that organizations have always had to operating in a volatile world. Those that survived, maintained their relevance, and created sustainability strategies offer a variety of lessons on the value of leveraging agility.

- *Trader Joe's and the vision of changing direction*: An American chain of grocery stores headquartered in Monrovia, California, and named after its founder, Joseph Hardin Coulombe. A few years after graduating college, Coulombe was hired by the Rexall drugstore chain, which tasked him with establishing a chain of convenience stores called Pronto. When Rexall lost interest in the stores, he was ordered to liquidate but instead decided to purchase the stores and

[19] Bose, T.K. 2010. *Total Quality of Management,* p. 99. Pearson. https://amazon. com/Total-Quality-Management-Tapan-Bose/dp/8131700224

rename them Pronto Markets. After the convenience store
chain, 7-Eleven entered the local market, Coulombe felt as
though Pronto Markets were too similar and he felt competition with 7-Eleven would be disastrous. In thinking about his
options, Coulombe recognized the necessity to do something
different. According to one interview Coulombe said, "*Scien-
tific American* had a story that of all people qualified to go to
college, 60 percent were going. I felt this newly educated—
not smarter but better-educated—class of people would
want something different, and that was the genesis of Trader
Joe's."[20] With Trader Joe's located near centers of learning
Coulombe positioned the stores "for overeducated and under-
paid people, for all the classical musicians, museum curators,
journalists."[21] Coulombe noted that such an approach proved
favorable in marketing and was "why we always had good
press, frankly!"[22] Coulombe founded Trader Joe's in 1967 and
he ran it until his retirement in 1988. He would eventually
sell Trader Joe's to Germany's Theo Albrecht (owner and CEO
of Aldi Nord) 1979. As of October 8, 2019, Trader Joe's had
504 stores in the United States.

- *TOMS and the lesson of an outdated vision*: While on vacation in Argentina in 2006, Blake Mycoskie met a woman,
  who was volunteering to deliver shoes to children. Mycoskie
  offered to help and has cited the shoe distribution experience,
  and the many shoeless children he encountered, as the birth
  of his idea for his eventual company. He launched TOMS
  Shoes LLC with a business model known as the "one for
  all concept" model, which is referring to the company's

[20] Genzlinger, N. 2020. "Joe Coulombe, Who Founded Trader Joe's, Dies at 89." *The New York Times*, February 29, 2020. https://nytimes.com/2020/02/29/business/joe-coulombe-dead.html

[21] Morrison, P. 2014. "Joe's Joe: Joe Coulombe." *Los Angeles Times*, March 15, 2014. https://latimes.com/opinion/la-oe-morrison-joe-coulombe-043011-column.html

[22] Morrison, P. 2014. "Joe's Joe: Joe Coulombe," *Los Angeles Times*, March 15, 2014. https://latimes.com/opinion/la-oe-morrison-joe-coulombe-043011-column.html

promise to deliver a pair of free shoes to a child in Argentina and other distressed locations upon the purchase of a retail pair of shoes. Since its inception, TOMS gifted close to 100 million pairs of shoes to children around the world. Unfortunately, the Los Angeles-based company has struggled to keep up with competitors lowering their prices, as the novelty of its "One for One" model of donating a pair of shoes for each one sold wears off among consumers. In 2018 Moody's reported a 10 percent decrease in overall annual revenues from $392 million for the 12 months ending June 2015.[23] The decline would continue with revenues dipping to $299 million for the 12 months ending June 30, 2019.[24] On December 27, 2019, TOMS Shoes LLC's creditors announced a takeover in exchange for restructuring its debt. Credit rating agencies had warned that TOMS would not have been able to repay a $300 million loan due next year without renegotiating it with its creditors.[25] While the company continues to donate shoes, its charitable model has evolved. It now says it commits a third of its net profits toward a giving fund that finances a wide range of philanthropic and social causes.

- *Adobe leverages technology to design its new vision*: Charles Geschke and John Warnock launched Adobe in 1982 and derived its name from nearby Adobe Creek in Los Altos,

[23] Biswas, S. 2018. "Toms Shoes Continues to See Shift to Online Sales." *Wall Street Journal*, May 29, 2018. https://wsj.com/articles/toms-shoes-continues-to-see-shift-to-online-sales-1527627965

[24] Collings, R. 2020. "With Restructuring, Toms Shoes Suffers Fate Common to Mall-Based Retailers." *AdWeek*, January 6, 2020. https://adweek.com/retail/with-restructuring-toms-shoes-suffers-fate-common-to-mall-based-retailers/

[25] Roumeliotis, G. 2019. "Exclusive: TOMS Shoes Creditors to take over the Company." *Reuters*, December 27, 2019. https://reuters.com/article/us-tomsshoes-m-a-creditors-exclusive/exclusive-toms-shoes-creditors-to-take-over-the-company-idUSKBN1YV1PT

California.[26] The original mission was to develop and sell the Post Script Language (PSL) used for printing documents on laser printers and very high-resolution printers. With Apple's inclusion of PSL for use in its LaserWriter printers in 1985, Adobe helped spark the desktop publishing revolution.[27] From the mid-1980s to mid-1990s, Adobe updated its mission by launching three innovative consumer software products: Illustrator, a vector-based drawing program for the Apple Macintosh, Photoshop, a graphics editing program, and PDF, the Portable Document Format, and its Adobe Acrobat and Reader software.[28] In 2012 Adobe updated its mission by transition from a provider of one-time purchase products (aka Creative Suite) to a true Software as a Service (SaaS) model. This "impressive move from a licensed software company to a completely cloud-based company" allowed designers to access Adobe's Creative Cloud and provided all of the software tools they needed without worrying about future updates.[29] As an agile manager in a volatile world, it is important to note that "this transition didn't happen overnight. Adobe had nearly 30 years of customer expectations to live up to, and a lot of users to convince that this was the right move. As a result, Adobe's evolution was carefully paced and comprehensive, effectively reshaping its core business model."[30]

- *Starbucks and the vision for a third place*: Howard Schultz made the third place—a location where people could gather outside

---

[26] "Adobe Corporation," *Silicon Valley Historical Association* https://siliconvalley-historical.org/adobe-corporation-history

[27] Scoble, R. 2011. "First look at Adobe Dreamweaver CS5.5 (better development of websites for mobile)," *Business Insider,* May 6, 2011. https://tinyurl.com/rkrnkho.

[28] "Adobe Corporation," *Silicon Valley Historical Association,* https://siliconvalleyhistorical.org/adobe-corporation-history

[29] "How Adobe Became a successful $95 billion SaaS company." https://producthabits.com/adobe-95-billion-saas-company/

[30] "7 Lessons from Adobe's Successful Transition to SaaS." May 28, 2019, *Bigfoot Capital.* https://tinyurl.com/vddqbu2

of the home or office—a significant part of society. While working as a general manager for a Swedish drip coffee maker manufacturer Hammarplast, Schultz visited one of his clients, a fledgling coffee-bean shop called Starbucks Coffee Company in Seattle in 1981. He kept in contact with the owners and a year later joined Starbucks as the director of marketing. As Schultz recalled, "in 1983, I was on a business trip to Italy when I walked into an Italian café and tasted my very first espresso. I was captivated by the beverage, the barista who prepared it and the romance of the café atmosphere."[31] This trip to Italy also provided him with the inspiration and vision that would become the bedrock of Starbucks. In addition to the excellent espresso, these Italian cafés served as meeting places or public squares; the 200,000 cafés in the country were an important element of Italian culture and society. At this time, Starbucks stores only sold whole bean coffee and had no seating. Schultz had the vision of creating specialty coffee stores that integrated the romance of espresso and provided a place for community."[32] The founders of Starbucks, however, were not interested so he went out on his own. With little personal money, he needed to tolerate over 200 rejections before investors gave him enough financing to launch his espresso bar Il Giornale. In 1987, the original owners sold the Starbucks chain to Schultz who rebranded his Il Giornale coffee outlets as Starbucks and quickly began to expand. What started out as a sleepy little coffee shop selling beans in 1971 has grown to operate over 31,000 locations worldwide in 2019 thanks to the vision of Howard Schultz.[33]

[31] Schultz, H. 2016. "A Dream 33 Years in the Making, Starbucks to open in Italy." https://stories.starbucks.com/stories/2016/howard-schultz-dream-fulfilled-starbucks-to-open-in-italy/

[32] Schultz, H. 2016. "A Dream 33 years in the Making, Starbucks to Open in Italy." https://stories.starbucks.com/stories/2016/howard-schultz-dream-fulfilled-starbucks-to-open-in-italy/

[33] "Number of international and United States Starbucks Stores from 2005 to 2019," Statista, https://statista.com/statistics/218366/number-of-international-and-us-starbucks-stores/

- *Ford and the vision of a blue ocean strategy:* The term "blue ocean" was coined by professors W. Chan Kim and Renee Mauborgne in their book *Blue Ocean Strategy: How to Create Uncontested Market Space and Make the Competition Irrelevant* (2005).[34] The authors define blue ocean strategy as the "simultaneous pursuit of differentiation and low cost to open up a new market space and create new demand. It is about creating and capturing uncontested market space"[35] Unlike red oceans that compete on price, the blue ocean allows an organization to make the competition irrelevant. The Ford Motor Company is one such example as it created a blue ocean in the automobile industry. In 1908 the first Model T cost $850, half the price of existing automobiles.[36] What's interesting to note for the agile manager is that hundreds of competitors existed. This red ocean found the products unreliable, small, and far too expensive. As Ford continued on its blue ocean strategy of making the competitor irrelevant, it dropped the price to $609 in 1909 and by 1924 it was down to $240.[37] Ford's success was underpinned by a profitable business model. By keeping the cars highly standardized and offering limited options and interchangeable parts, Ford's revolutionary assembly line replaced skilled craftsmen with ordinary unskilled laborers who worked one small task faster and more efficiently, cutting the labor hours by 60 percent. With lower costs, Ford was able to charge a price that was accessible to the mass market.

---

[34] *Blue Ocean Strategy: How to Create Uncontested Market Space and Make the Competition Irrelevant.* 2005. https://tinyurl.com/u3yr9tr

[35] Definition located at https://blueoceanstrategy.com/what-is-blue-ocean-strategy/

[36] Blue Ocean Strategy Examples, June 13, 2017. https://blueoceansys.com/blogs/blue-ocean-strategy-examples/

[37] Blue Ocean Strategy Examples, June 13, 2017. https://blueoceansys.com/blogs/blue-ocean-strategy-examples/

Agile managers in a volatile world should recognize the limitation of curating ideas. The function of the curator is a necessity but unless the agile manager functions as an architect it will be nearly impossible for the organization to become more agile. The manager as architect needs to acknowledge that mission (foundation), vision (façade), and values (design) are three separate, yet interrelated components of a dynamic entity. Business history is littered with managers who failed to serve in the function of a curator that, in turn, then flopped as an architect. Consider the following examples: Xerox decided to not take Canon's entry into the personal copiers seriously, Kodak became blind to the rise of digital photography, and Sears never found a way to compete effectively with Walmart. In each case, as with hundreds more, the senior management team lacked the will, vision, and agility to maintain the organization's relevance. Even when and where a manager had an idea, they lacked follow-through.[38] To help translate ideas into action the agile manager can cultivate an organization's values (Principle #6).

Principle #6: Cultivate Values

The sixth principle of cultivating values is the third component in the architect function of the agile manager with updating the mission (Principle #4) and designing the vision (Principle #5) as the other two. The interrelatedness of mission, vision, and values will only continue to serve as a critical junction for agile managers to work on in a volatile world increasingly marked by a hyperconnected global customer base. "Company culture," wrote Mengqi Sun in *The Wall Street Journal*, "is becoming more of a touchpoint for investors and customers, who are increasingly taking corporate behavior into consideration when choosing products or services."[39] The advent and growth of social media during the last decade has magnified the significance of organizational behavior,

---

[38] Govindarajan, V. 2010. "Innovation is not creativity," *Harvard Business Review*, August 3, 2010. https://hbr.org/2010/08/innovation-is-not-creativity.html

[39] Sun, M. 2019. "Papa John's Looks to Improve Corporate Culture After Founder Flap." *The Wall Street Journal*, March 1, 2019. https://wsj.com/articles/papa-johns-looks-to-improve-corporate-culture-after-founder-flap-11551477189

values, and culture. Amazon is just one example of many. On April 22, 2018, Amazon CEO and founder Jeff Bezos was on vacation and tweeted about dog sledding in Norway. For an organization often accused of poor warehouse conditions to employee strikes over low wages, this caused quit the stir on social media with people commenting on such an extravagant trip. Comedian Sarah Silverman reminded the entrepreneur about his employees who depend on food stamps and government assistance.[40]

In response to the criticism about its values, Amazon raised the minimum wages of its U.S. warehouse workers to $15 in October 2018.[41] Despite the influential role that values and ethical leadership play in developing robust organizational cultures, research findings in this report reveal that employees around the world are not seeing enough evidence of either of these elements. *The Impact of Organizational Values and Ethical Leadership on Misconduct: A Global Look: 2019 Global Business Ethics Survey* found 39 percent of employees do not see a strong commitment to organizational values in their organization while 58 percent of employees do not see a strong commitment to ethical leadership in their organization.[42] Over the last few years, managers looking to demonstrate such a commitment have developed policies around corporate social responsibility (CSR). In a volatile world what is the manager's approach to corporate social responsibility? This principle deserves consideration following the Business Roundtable's *Statement on the Purpose of a Corporation* on August 19, 2019 declaring, "Americans deserve an economy that allows each person to succeed through hard work and creativity and to lead a life

---

[40] Matyszczyk, C. 2018. "Amazon CEO Jeff Bezos Showed Off his Exciting Vacation on Twitter. What Happened Next Wasn't Pretty." *Inc.* April 23, 2018. https://inc.com/chris-matyszczyk/amazon-ceo-jeff-bezos-showed-off-his-exciting-vacation-on-twitter-what-happened-next-wasnt-pretty.html

[41] Salinas, S. 2018. "Amazon Raises Minimum Wage to $15 for all US Employees." *CNBC*, October 2, 2018. https://cnbc.com/2018/10/02/amazon-raises-minimum-wage-to-15-for-all-us-employees.html

[42] "The Impact of Organizational Values and Ethical Leadership on Misconduct: A Global Look: 2019 Global Business Ethics Survey." https://43wli92bfqd835mbif2ms9qz-wpengine.netdna-ssl.com/wp-content/uploads/2019-GBES-for-Release.pdf

of meaning and dignity."[43] Such a proclamation moved corporate social responsibility, a topic long placed in the background, into the forefront of business discussions in the United States. In his 1953 publication *Social Responsibilities of the Businessman*, American economist Howard Bowen coined the term "corporate social responsibility" (CSR).[44] The practice of CSR continued to evolve during the next few decades as more organizations included social interests in their business practices while becoming more responsive to employees, customers, and other stakeholders.[45] While sporadic efforts were made during the 1980s and 1990s, the oft quoted phrase "Greed is right, greed works. Greed clarifies, cuts through, and captures the essence of the evolutionary spirit" by Michael Douglas in the 1987 film *Wall Street,* signified the *Weltanschauung* of the times.

It was not until 1999, however, that CSR gained global attention with the landmark speech of then Secretary General of the United Nations, Kofi Annan, who at the World Economic Forum, said: "I propose that you, the business leaders gathered in Davos, and we, the United Nations, initiate a global compact of shared values and principles, which will give a human face to the global market"[46] Annan's speech launched the United Nations Global Compact (UNGC) on July 2000 involving 44 global companies, 6 business associations, and 2 labor and 12 civil society organizations. In the 2019 report *Leading the Social Enterprise: Reinvent with a Human Focus* by Deloitte a social enterprise is defined as "an organization whose mission combines revenue growth and profit-making with the need to respect and

[43] Business Roundtable Redefines the Purpose of a Corporation to Promote "An Economy That Serves All Americans" August 19, 2019. https://tinyurl.com/v8w4e7u

[44] Agudelo, L., M.A., L. Jóhannsdóttir, and B. Davídsdóttir. 2019. "A Literature Review of the History and Evolution of Corporate Social Responsibility." *Int J Corporate Soc Responsibility* 4, no. 1 https://doi.org/10.1186/s40991-018-0039-y

[45] A Brief History of Corporate Social Responsibility (CSR), September 25, 2019. https://thomasnet.com/insights/history-of-corporate-social-responsibility/

[46] Agudelo, L., M.A., L. Jóhannsdóttir, and B. Davídsdóttir. 2019. "A Literature Review of the History and Evolution of Corporate Social Responsibility." *Int J Corporate Soc Responsibility* 4, no. 1. https://doi.org/10.1186/s40991-018-0039-y

support its environment and stakeholder network."[47] To that end, today's social enterprise needs agile managers who understand the value of "listening to, investing in, and actively managing the trends that are shaping today's world while helping the organization be a good citizen (both inside and outside the organization), serving as a role model for its peers and promoting a high degree of collaboration at every level of the organization."[48] Giving by corporations is estimated to have increased by 5.4 percent in 2018, totaling $20.05 billion (an increase of 2.9 percent, adjusted for inflation).[49] Those companies know that investing in social responsibility programs generates huge potential benefits, such as increasing revenue up to 20 percent or reducing employee turnover rate by up to 50 percent. There is an expectation now that companies engage in social responsibility programs since 87 percent of customers expect companies to do more than make a profit.[50] Also known as the triple-P approach to governance, organizations are asked to be mindful of profit, people, and planet.

Once such formal process is complete, the agile manager might consider is certifying the organization as a Certified B Corporation verified by B Lab, a nonprofit organization. "B Lab certifies companies based on how they create value for non-shareholding stakeholders, such as their employees, the local community, and the environment. Once a firm crosses a certain performance threshold on these dimensions, it makes amendments to its corporate charter to incorporate the interests of all stakeholders into the fiduciary duties of directors and officers."[51] Most B

---

[47] Deloitte. "Leading the Social Enterprise: Reinvent with a Human Focus." 2019 Deloitte Global Human Capital Trends, https://www2.deloitte.com/content/dam/Deloitte/cz/Documents/human-capital/cz-hc-trends-reinvent-with-human-focus.pdf

[48] Deloitte. "Leading the Social Enterprise: Reinvent with a Human Focus." 2019 Deloitte Global Human Capital Trends, https://www2.deloitte.com/content/dam/Deloitte/cz/Documents/human-capital/cz-hc-trends-reinvent-with-human-focus.pdf

[49] Giving USA 2019, https://givingusa.org

[50] "B Impact Report." *Valor CSR*, https://bcorporation.net/directory/valor-csr

[51] Kim, S., et. al. 2016. "Why Companies are Becoming B Corporations." *Harvard Business Review,* June 17, 2016. https://hbr.org/2016/06/why-companies-are-becoming-b-corporations

Corporations are privately held small and medium-sized businesses. The first generation of B Corporations was certified in 2007 and exceeded 1,700 in 50 countries by 2016. As the cofounders of B Lap noted, "The B Corp Movement is playing a leadership role by inspiring and empowering millions of people to change their buying behavior and creating advocates who can build new institutions, demand more for their money, and create the necessary policy changes to accelerate this shift."[52] Becoming B certified is merely one option for the agile manager to cultivate the organizations values and demonstrate its corporate social responsibility. As an agile manager, one has other options to cultivate values in addition to engaging in corporate social responsibility or becoming B certified. A consistent adherence to specific values is available to any manager of an organization. The privately held restaurant Chick-fil-A provides an excellent case study in the consistent adherence to organizational values.

Now with over 2,300 locations, Chick-fil-A had stood out among organizations for its strong and consistent dedication to its values during the last six decades. The privately held company is known by its slogan "We didn't invent the chicken, just the chicken sandwich," its waffle fries, dedication to the local community, and being closed on Sundays among so many other characteristics. This value of being closed on Sundays started in 1946 when brothers Ben and Truett Cathy opened their first restaurant, the Dwarf Grill, outside Atlanta, Georgia.[53] Cultivating the value of being closed on Sunday continued when Truett opened his first Chick-fil-A in 1967. "My brother Ben and I closed our restaurant on the first Sunday after we opened in 1946," Truett said, "and my children have committed to closing our restaurants on Sundays long after I'm gone." Truett passed away in September 2014 and sure enough, all 2,300 plus restaurants are still closed on Sunday; carrying on the tradition that started back in 1946. In his book *Eat Mor Chikin: Inspire More People,*

---

[52] Gilbert, C., B. Houlahan, and A. Kassoy. 2015. "What is the Role of Business in Society?" *The Aspen Institute*, November 10, 2015. https://aspeninstitute.org/blog-posts/what-role-business-society/

[53] "History of Chick-fil-A Located on Chick-fil-A." Website at https://chick-fil-a.com/about/history

Truett wrote, "Closing our business on Sunday, the Lord's Day, is our way of honoring God and showing our loyalty to Him." Even as it expanded nationwide, Chick-fil-A remained a distinctly Southern institution, one that generated fierce loyalty among its customers. In 1982, the company adopted a two-sentence corporate mission: "To glorify God by being a faithful steward of all that is entrusted to us. To have a positive influence on all who come in contact with Chick-fil-A."[54]

Commenting on Chick-fil-A's decision to cultivate its values by remaining closed on Sundays, John Hamburger, the president of *Franchise Times,* noted such a move was a counterintuitive sales booster. "Being open six days provides benefits to both the operators and the customers," Hamburger said. "The owner-operator gets the time off. 'Closed on Sunday' conveys a sense of caring and community to the customers."[55] To maintain a strong sense of community built upon a foundation of long-standing values, Truett decided to keep Chick-fil-A private and not succumb to the "expedient Wall Street way of doing things."[56] Going public for the prospect of an even bigger payday never persuaded Truett to stray from his values.[57] Doing so, he said in a 1998 interview, would mean giving up family control of matters such as contributions to charity and remaining closed on Sundays. "As a public company, I'm sure somebody

[54] Arnold, L. 2014. "Truett Cathy, Chick-fil-A Founder, dies at 93." *Washington Post,* September 8, 2014. https://washingtonpost.com/local/obituaries/truett-cathy-founder-of-chik-fil-a-dies-at-93/2014/09/08/638db948-3768-11e4-9c9f-ebb47272e40e_story.html

[55] Taylor, K. 2019. "Chick-fil-A Likely Loses Out on more than $1 billion in Sales Every Year by Closing on Sundays—and It's a Brilliant Business Strategy." *Business Insider,* July 29, 2019. https://businessinsider.com/chick-fil-a-closes-on-sunday-why-2019-7

[56] Taylor, K. 2019. "Chick-fil-A Likely Loses Out on More than $1 Billion in Sales Every Year by Closing on Sundays—and It's a Brilliant Business Strategy." *Business Insider,* July 29, 2019. https://businessinsider.com/chick-fil-a-closes-on-sunday-why-2019-7

[57] Arnold, L. 2014. "Truett Cathy, Chick-fil-A founder, dies at 93." *Washington Post,* September 8, 2014. https://washingtonpost.com/local/obituaries/truett-cathy-founder-of-chik-fil-a-dies-at-93/2014/09/08/638db948-3768-11e4-9c9f-ebb47272e40e_story.html

would object to our generosity," he said.[58] Such values-driven generosity, however, has had a positive impact on the organization's bottom line.

By sticking to his values, Truett understood Chick-fil-A willingly surrenders more than $1 billion in annual sales by closing on Sundays. And, for Chick-fil-A, it's worth it as sales continue to increase.[59] Today, Chick-fil-A is the third largest chain in the United States by sales, growing revenue by 16.7 percent in 2018 to reach nearly $10.5 billion. Even though it is closed one day a week, the average Chick-fil-A unit made more in 2017 than a McDonald's, Starbucks, and Subway combined. The average Chick-fil-A made approximately $4,090,900 in 2017. By contrast, the total sales for a McDonald's ($2,670,320 per unit), Starbucks ($945,270), and Subway ($416,860) was $4,032,450.[60] By cultivating a strong sense of values for decades, Chick-fil-A's policy of remaining closed on Sundays provides all employees to a day off, demonstrates how a manager can stay true to principles while increasing the bottom line. In today's volatile world, balancing both values and profits is needed now more than ever.

The second function of the agile manager as architect examined the need to update the mission (Principle #4), define a vision (Principle #5), and cultivate values (Principle #6). Once the three separate yet interrelated components of mission (foundation), vision (façade), and values (design) are in place, one can shift from architect to conductor—the third function of the agile manager. The Weber Shandwick/KRC Research report *The State of Corporate Reputation in 2020: Everything Matters Now* illustrates the very need for agile managers to function as a conductor when it concluded: "global executives attribute 63 percent of their company's

---

[58] Arnold, L. 2014. "Truett Cathy, Chick-fil-A founder, dies at 93," *Washington Post,* September 8, 2014. https://washingtonpost.com/local/obituaries/truett-cathy-founder-of-chik-fil-a-dies-at-93/2014/09/08/638db948-3768-11e4-9c9f-ebb47272e40e_story.html

[59] Taylor, K. 2019. "The Church of Chicken: The Inside Story of How Chick-Fil-A Used Christian Values and a 'Clone Army' to Build a Booming Business that's Defying the Retail Apocalypse and Taking over America." *Business Insider,* August 8, 2019. https://businessinsider.com/how-chick-fil-a-took-over-america-2019-8

[60] McCreary, M. "Chick-fil-A Makes More Per Restaurant than McDonald's, Starbucks and Subway combined ... and It's Closed on Sundays." *Entrepreneur* magazine, https://entrepreneur.com/article/320615

market value to their company's overall reputation."[61] As a conductor, the agile manager ensures the collaboration, skill development, and relationship building required to synchronize the organization's reputation with its mission, vision, and values.

Questions

Principle #4: Update Mission

- How do you know if everyone understands your organization's mission?
- Where is the organization's mission displayed publicly?
- How often do you refer to your mission?
- How often do your employees refer to the mission?
- Does your organization need to update its mission?
- Does the business model of your organization need to be reinvented?
- What skills, traits, or habits can you rely on to help you become more agile as you prepare for an unknown future?
- How comfortable are you becoming irrelevant?
- What are you going to do to help your organization remain relevant?

Principle #5: Design Vision

- How often do you talk about vision?
- When you do talk about vision do you include others in its development?
- How comfortable are you discussing vision publicly?
- How often do you think about corporate social responsibility?
- As an agile manager, what do you think you can do to help promote CSR?

---

[61] "The State of Corporate Reputation in 2020: Everything Matters Now." January 14, 2020. https://webershandwick.com/news/corporate-reputation-2020-everything-matters-now/

- What skills, traits, or habits can you rely on to design, or redesign, a vision for an organization in a volatile world?
- Which vision story resonates with you the most and why?
- What lessons can you learn from the TOMS story?
- How familiar are you with blue ocean strategies?
- Why do you think organizations find it easy to generate a new idea but difficult to implement it?

Principle #6: Cultivate Values

- What would employees identify as the top five values of your organization?
- What do you think the organization values most?
- How often do you reflect upon your organization's culture?
- What have you done to update your organization's responsibility to its people and surrounding community?
- What values would you like to improve upon in your organization?
- As an agile manager in a volatile world, how can you help cultivate values?
- What has been the impact of external events on your organization's culture?
- How has your organization leveraged its values to navigate difficult times?
- How does your organization's social media presence reflect its values?

CHAPTER 5

Conductor

Introduction to Function #3: Conductor

The third function of an agile manager is that of a conductor ensuring collaboration, skill development, and harmony among internal constituents and between the organization and external stakeholders and partners. Fostering collaboration across departments, functional areas, and offices illustrates a critical component of agility. (Principle #7). Managers also need to demonstrate a commitment to ensuring employees receiving the skill development, training, and education required to succeed (Principle #8). Such collaboration and skill development prepares the organization to as the agile manager nurtures relationships with external stakeholders (Principle #9). Previous references to the manager as conductor include Sune Carlson's 1951 *Executive Behavior*, Peter Drucker's 1954 *The Practice of Management* and Len Sayles' 1964 *Managerial Behavior*. Carlson referred to the chief executive as the conductor of an orchestra who was "the puppet in the puppet-show with hundreds of people pulling the strings and forcing him to act in one way or another. Drucker believed "the manager is both composer and conductor." Sayles observed "the manager is like a symphony orchestra conductor, endeavoring to maintain a melodious performance."[1]

The reference to manager as conductor in this publication offers a more current adaptation of the oft-used analogy. The function of the manager as conductor refers to the skills, habits, and traits of a manager required to conduct the level of collaboration required of an agile organization. Any progress away from antiquity (the usual way of doing things) and to modernity (a new, creative, and agile approach) demands a manager who can direct his behavior, and that of others, in the required direction forward. The function

---

[1] Mintzberg, H. 2016. "The Maestro Myth of Managing." April 28, 2016. https://mintzberg.org/blog/conductor

of an agile manager as conductor exceeds the works of Carlson, Drucker, and Sayles. The agile organization demands a manager who carves his own path (not a puppet as per Carlson) provides vision where there is darkness (more than a composer and conductor per Drucker) and maintains focus on relevance, vibrancy, and vitality (and not worrying about a melodious performance as per Sayles). The agile manager as conductor requires a high level of self-awareness, a dedication to continuous personal growth, and a recognition that professional development is linked to personal growth. If one wants to grow as a professional and transform into an agile manager, one needs to grow as a person and help others in the organization do the same. The agile manager as conductor should understand the role of the organization's human capital during times of high change, volatility, complexity, and ambiguity. When developed properly, an organization's human capital can leverage agility and collaborate across functional areas, departments, and skill sets to solve business issues, answer critical questions, and address key issues to ensure positive business outcomes.[2] As PricewaterCoopers noted in its 2020 report *23rd Annual Global CEO Survey: Navigating the Rising Tide of Uncertainty*, "when it comes to the most pressing topics confronting CEOs, collaboration between and among organizations, individuals and governments can meaningfully enhance not only their own prospects but the prosperity and vitality of society as a whole."[3]

Principle #7: Foster Collaboration

The challenge to foster collaboration is getting more acute as today's VUCA global marketplace continues to change the fabric of how we live and work.[4] As world issues such as global warming, pandemics, and

---

[2] Llopis, G. 2018. "HR Departments must Urgently Become Human Capital Departments." *Forbes*, January 8, 2018. https://forbes.com/sites/glennllopis/2018/01/08/hr-departments-must-urgently-become-human-capital-departments/#11b9bcd421a6

[3] PwC. "23rd Annual Global CEO Survey: Navigating the Rising Tide of Uncertainty." 2020 edition. https://pwc.com/gx/en/ceo-survey/2020/reports/pwc-23rd-global-ceo-survey.pdf

[4] McKinsey & Company. 2016. "Making Collaboration Across Functions a Reality." March 2016. https://mckinsey.com/business-functions/organization/our-insights/making-collaboration-across-functions-a-reality

geopolitical upheaval intensify, "it's increasingly apparent that we'll need coordinated teams to get things done."[5] Collaboration has long been a tool in the armamentarium of organizational effectiveness, however, and continues to evolve.[6] The agile manager looking to foster collaboration needs to understand doing so requires some knowledge about people, roles, technology, workplaces, processes, communication, interactions, negotiations, processes, and a variety of other factors.[7] An agile organization demonstrating higher levels of collaboration can provide opportunities to maintain and increase a competitive advantage.[8] For example, research has found companies with a mature innovation process were more likely to have innovation activities integrated or collaborating with their strategy (81 percent vs. 56 percent), corporate development/M&A (48 percent vs. 29 percent), and corporate venture capital (62 percent vs. 30 percent) teams, when compared to other organizations.[9] As McKinsey noted, "working collaboratively can be a powerful enabler of improved business performance, but successful collaboration rarely emerges out of the blue and should not be taken for granted."[10]

One research project reported nearly 75 percent of cross-functional teams are dysfunctional defined as failing on at least three of the following

---

[5] Puybaraud, M., and K. Kristensen. 2020. "Collaboration 2020: Hype or Competitive Advantage." *Johnson Controls*, www.profacility.be/piclib/biblio/PDF_00000543UK.pdf

[6] Puybaraud, M., and K. Kristensen. 2020. "Collaboration 2020: Hype or Competitive Advantage." *Johnson Controls*, www.profacility.be/piclib/biblio/PDF_00000543UK.pdf

[7] Puybaraud, M., and K. Kristensen. 2020. "Collaboration 2020: Hype or Competitive Advantage." *Johnson Controls*, www.profacility.be/piclib/biblio/PDF_00000543UK.pdf

[8] "How to Foster More Effective Team Collaboration and Communications." *Mitel blog*, February 9, 2018. https://mitel.com/blog/how-to-foster-more-effective-team-collaboration-and-communications

[9] KPMG. "Benchmarking Innovation Impact 2020." https://info.kpmg.us/content/dam/info/en/innovation-enterprise-solutions/pdf/2019/benchmarking-innovation-impact-2020.pdf

[10] Puybaraud, M., and K. Kristensen. 2020. "Collaboration 2020: Hype or Competitive Advantage." *Johnson Controls*, www.profacility.be/piclib/biblio/PDF_00000543UK.pdf

five criteria: (1) meeting a planned budget; (2) staying on schedule; (3) adhering to specifications; (4) meeting customer expectations; and/or (5) maintaining alignment with the company's corporate goals.[11] A lack of collaboration is often the hallmark of such dysfunction and results in unclear governance, a lack of accountability, and an organizational failure to prioritize and implement strategic imperatives.[12] So why is fostering collaboration so difficult? One problem is managers fail to create the necessary alliances required to resolve the internal conflicts and resource debates often found in collaboration initiatives.[13] Another issue is leaders think about collaboration as a value to cultivate but not a skill to teach. This narrow approach has included superficial or heavy-handed policies such as open offices to naming collaboration an official corporate goal.[14] While many of these approaches yield progress, research has shown truly robust collaboration requires other sophisticated and agile measures.[15]

In their pursuit of collaboration, the nonagile manager focuses on logistics and processes, incentives and outcomes. In today's volatile world, achieving and sustaining growth is a critical priority so focusing on outcomes makes perfect sense. Such an approach, however, fails to consider the implications related to collaboration on a human capital level. In its simplest form, collaboration involves people working together. Understanding, predicting, and supporting how employees might react when

---

[11] Tabrizi, B. 2015. "75% of Cross-Functional Teams are Dysfunctional." *Harvard Business Review,* June 23, 2015. https://hbr.org/2015/06/75-of-cross-functional-teams-are-dysfunctional

[12] Tabrizi, B. 2015. "75% of Cross-Functional Teams are Dysfunctional." *Harvard Business Review,* June 23, 2015. https://hbr.org/2015/06/75-of-cross-functional-teams-are-dysfunctional

[13] KPMG. "Benchmarking Innovation Impact 2020." https://info.kpmg.us/content/dam/info/en/innovation-enterprise-solutions/pdf/2019/benchmarking-innovation-impact-2020.pdf

[14] Gino, F. 2019. "Cracking the Code of Sustained Collaboration." *Harvard Business Review,* November-December 2019. https://hbr.org/2019/11/cracking-the-code-of-sustained-collaboration

[15] Gino, F. 2019. "Cracking the Code of Sustained Collaboration." *Harvard Business Review,* November-December 2019. https://hbr.org/2019/11/cracking-the-code-of-sustained-collaboration

any measure of agility is implemented remains critical for the agile manager. Asking people to engage in the common hallmarks of collaboration: break down walls, divulge information, sacrifice autonomy, share resources, and possibly even cede responsibilities could send unintended messages and derail important collaborative efforts.[16]

Moreover, employees, board members, and even clients could feel vulnerable, threatened, or even irrelevant.[17] Proceed with caution; but do indeed proceed. The agile manager as a conductor who fosters collaboration needs to increase their self-awareness in order to engage in the highest level of empathy required to ensure people continue to feel as valuable members of the organization during times of collaboration initiatives. As David Aycan, Managing Director, IDEO Products, concluded, "if their work does not seem important, employees will detach mentally and emotionally. When leaders design work environments with their teams' needs in mind, they are more likely to be engaged and willing to adopt new, better behaviors."[18] Moreover, the integration of automated systems, robotics, and artificial intelligence into an organization's collaboration efforts will push the agile manager's skills to new levels. As the Institute for the Future reported, "we will be entering into a new kind of partnership with machines that will build on our mutual strengths, resulting in a new level of human–machine collaboration and codependence."[19]

To foster effective collaboration, the agile manager can look to a theme repeated throughout history and most recently detailed in a 1953 article by British scholar Isaiah Berlin regarding "The Hedgehog and the Fox." Attributed to the Ancient Greek poet Archilochus who postulated

---

[16] Kwan, L.B. 2019. "The Collaboration Blind Spot." *Harvard Business Review,* March–April 2019. https://hbr.org/2019/03/the-collaboration-blind-spot

[17] Kwan, L.B. 2019. "The Collaboration Blind Spot." *Harvard Business Review,* March–April 2019. https://hbr.org/2019/03/the-collaboration-blind-spot

[18] Aycan, D. 2019. "Innovation Thrives Under These 5 Evidence-Backed Conditions." *Innovation Leader,* November 2019. https://d22yapd4ylp3wi.cloudfront.net/Uploads/w/x/w/pointersnovember2019_11_20_2019_198008.pdf

[19] Institute for the Future, *Future Work Skills 2020,* www.iftf.org/uploads/media/SR-1382A_UPRI_future_work_skills_sm.pdf

"a fox knows many things, but a hedgehog one important thing") and echoed in *Adagia* by Erasmus in 1500. Berlin divided writers and thinkers into two categories: hedgehogs, who view the world through the lens of a single defining idea (examples include Plato, Friedrich Nietzsche, and Marcel Proust), and foxes, who draw on a wide variety of experiences and for whom the world cannot be boiled down to a single idea (examples include Aristotle, Johann Wolfgang Goethe, and James Joyce). When applied to organizational behavior, culture, and operations hedgehogs are employees who have deep experience in one narrow field or experts in a specific subject matter.

Foxes, however, have jumped from discipline to discipline to learn many things—yet followed no neat trajectory (and are unsure trajectories even exist). Hedgehogs bring deep domain expertise and the increasing complexity of our workplaces has placed an understandable premium on their concentrated mastery. Conversely, the natural habitat of foxes is innovation, which depends on the ability to mix preexisting and often widely divergent elements into a new creative combination. The research suggests that hedgehogs are common while foxes are a rare sight but in high demand. As *Boston Globe* writer David Dabscheck observed, "the resulting scarcity of foxlike thinking has led to a predictable gap between the professed desire for innovation and results."[20] As the agile manager fosters collaboration, they would serve themselves and their organization well by increasing their self-awareness in order to be more fox like.

Scott Kirsner, CEO and Co-Founder of Innovation Leader, commented on the imperative of collaboration and noted "teams need to find ways to collaborate with other parts of the organization because there are always internal conflicts and resource debates you'll need to work through."[21] For the agile manager operating in a volatile world, confliction resolution will be an inevitable component of any collaboration efforts.

---

[20] Dabscheck, D. 2014. "Silicon Valley Needs More Foxes." *Boston Globe,* September 21, 2014. https://bostonglobe.com/opinion/2014/09/20/for-innovation-silicon-valley-needs-more-foxes/VhYrFOY43orE2VmSDQ5sNI/story.html
[21] KPMG. "Benchmarking Innovation Impact 2020." https://info.kpmg.us/content/dam/info/en/innovation-enterprise-solutions/pdf/2019/benchmarking-innovation-impact-2020.pdf

So too is the need to educate, train, and reskill employees. The function of the agile manager as conductor involves collaboration (Principle #7) and training (Principle #8). New technology will continue to alter how people work, what they do, and where they do it. Organizations will need a commitment to agility and adapt to the new means of work or risk irrelevance. And employees will need to engage in lifelong learning in order to maintain the relevant skills required of work in a volatile world. "Blue-collar jobs will be replaced by 'new collar' jobs that require a combination of digital, technical, and soft skills."[22] Finding people with the right combination of skills persists as an underlying concern for many organizations. In one survey, 41 percent of respondents had trouble recruiting talent with high-demand skillsets as the biggest obstacle their organizations face.[23]

Principle #8: Commit to Development

Ensuring a commitment to employee development through proper skill development, training, and education (Principle #8) is another component of the conductor function of the agile manager. While providing the leadership to help departments collaborate (Principle #7) providing the required learning opportunities for employees to do their jobs, or perhaps a new one, requires the agile manager to remain ever vigilant on human capital trends. Recognizing the disruptive political, regulatory, and technological forces impacting the financial services industries, Pricewater-Coopers (PwC) published *The Power to Perform: Human Capital 2020 and Beyond* in 2020 and noted the need for new skills, an agile mindset, and creative ways of attracting, motivating, and organizing employees. Addressing these three critical issues, according to the report, can help

---

[22] PwC, *23rd Annual Global CEO Survey: Navigating the Rising Tide of Uncertainty*, 2020 edition. https://pwc.com/gx/en/ceo-survey/2020/reports/pwc-23rd-global-ceo-survey.pdf

[23] KPMG. "Benchmarking Innovation Impact 2020." https://info.kpmg.us/content/dam/info/en/innovation-enterprise-solutions/pdf/2019/benchmarking-innovation-impact-2020.pdf

organizations ensure they have the human capital needed to succeed.[24] IBM's 2019 report *The Enterprise Guide to Closing the Skills Gap* suggests 120 million workers worldwide will need to be retrained as a result of artificial intelligence, automation, and other disruptive technologies.[25] McKinsey's research suggests approximately 3 percent of the global workforce, approximately 90 million workers, will need to change occupational categories by 2030.[26] The reports from PwC, IBM, and McKinsey, as well as a host of others, ranked agility as a top soft skill and discuss the need for managers to maintain a vigilance toward employee development through proper skill development, training, and education.[27] Much of the focus of employee training today centers around leaders from businesses, organizations, and government offices around the world racing to figure out how to balance employee training between hard skills and soft skills required for their organization to achieve and sustain growth.

Hard skills are teachable and measurable abilities often learned in classrooms and may require a college degree. For some employment positions, a graduate degree is required. Common hard skills employers look for today are artificial intelligence, automation, bilingual or multilingual, database management, network security, data analytics, SEO/SEM marketing, and computer programming. Soft skills, on the other hand, are more difficult to measure, are seldom learned in classrooms, and certainly do not require a college degree. While there are many employment positions that require little to no hard skills, almost every job requires the employee to have some level of proficiency regarding soft skills. Frequently cited soft skills mentioned by employers are

---

[24] PwC. "The Power to Perform: Human Capital 2020 and Beyond." https://pwchk.com/en/financial-services/fs-human-capital-2020.pdf

[25] IBM. 2019. "The Enterprise Guide to Closing the Skills Gap." https://ibm.com/downloads/cas/EPYMNBJA

[26] Manyika, J., and K. Sneader. 2018. "AI, Automation, and the Future of Work: Ten Things to Solve For." *McKinsey Global Institute*, June 2018. https://mckinsey.com/featured-insights/future-of-work/ai-automation-and-the-future-of-work-ten-things-to-solve-for

[27] "Agility is Today's Key Soft Skill for Success." *Canadian Immigrant*, July 9, 2018. https://canadianimmigrant.ca/careers-and-education/softskills/agility-is-todays-key-soft-skill-for-success

self-awareness, empathy, integrity, dependability, communication, team-work, agility, problem-solving, open-mindedness, and adaptability to name a few. In her book *The Hard Truth about Soft Skills*, Peggy Klaus defined the difference "While hard skills refer to the technical ability and the factual knowledge needed to do the job, soft skills allow you to more effectively use your technical abilities and knowledge. Soft skills encompass personal, social, communication, and self-management behaviors."[28]

The agile manager in a volatile world needs to understand hard skills are not harder to learn; nor are soft skills less important because softness is interpreted as a weakness when juxtaposed to hard. Perhaps an easy reference point is the application of objective and subjective. Hard skills generally require one to pass an objective test. For example, a manager either knows how to create a pivot table in Excel and analyze the data accordingly or they lack the ability to do so. Objective tests measure in either or. Soft skills, however, require a much more subjective assessment measure and are far more difficult to quantify like hard skills. For example, IBM's 2019 report found willingness to be flexible, agile, and adaptable to change went from number three to number one on the list of behavioral skills identified as the most critical for members of the workforce today by executives.[29] Reaching any degree of consensus on defining agility would be difficult even for the most collaborative of teams. Assessing agility as a soft skill would prove even more problematic. Guided self-awareness exercises through reflection, role-playing, and dialogue are common learning modalities used to help people increase their soft skills.

The agile manager should understand a volatile world upends business practices and demands they go through continuous evolution. Technological innovations such as automation, robotics, and artificial intelligence (AI) will drive this evolutionary process creating a future of

---

[28] Klaus, P. 2008. *The Hard Truth about Soft Skills: Workplace Lessons Smart People Wish They'd Learned Soone.* Harper Business. https://amazon.com/Hard-Truth-About-Soft-Skills/dp/0061284149

[29] IBM. "The Enterprise Guide to Closing the Skills Gap," 2019. https://ibm.com/downloads/cas/EPYMNBJA

work requiring a high degree of proficiency with soft skills. As Ken Taylor wrote in *Training Industry* "even with this transformation, soft skills like creativity, agile thinking, communication and collaboration will stay in high demand." [30] Agile managers understand the research and realize the employees who endure the evolutionary changes to the business practices of the organization maintain a commitment to improve their soft skills.[31] Such dedication to enhancing soft skills requires persistent effort over an extended period of time, an increase in self-awareness, and a willingness to be vulnerable because invariably constructive criticism of one's behavior needs to be included in training. Rest assured though, developing soft skills pays tremendous dividends across positions, levels, and industries.

Research conducted with Fortune 500 CEOs by the Stanford Research Institute International and the Carnegie Melon Foundation, found that 75 percent of long-term job success depends on people skills, while only 25 percent on technical knowledge.[32] Klaus echoed similar sentiment in her book *The Hard Truth about Soft Skills* and wrote "75 percent of long-term job success depends on people skills, while only 25 percent on technical knowledge."[33] One example of this emphasis on soft skills as a leading indicator of long-term job success comes from the Graduate Management Admission Council (GMAC). In a survey of MBA graduates, the GMAC reported individuals strong in analytical aptitude, quantitative expertise, and information-gathering ability but weak in the critical areas of great value to employers: strategic thinking, written and

---

[30]   Taylor, K. 2019. "Trends 2020: the Broadening Role of L&D." *Training Industry,* November/December 2019. https://trainingindustry.com/magazine/nov-dec-2019/trends-2020-the-broadening-role-of-ld/

[31]   Liu, J. 2020. "The 3 Most Important Skills Workers Need to Learn in 2020, According to Business Leaders." *Make It,* March 3, 2020. https://cnbc.com/2020/03/03/linkedin-report-3-most-important-skills-workers-need-to-learn-in-2020.html

[32]   American Management Association. "The Hard Truth about Soft Skills." January 24, 2019. https://amanet.org/articles/the-hard-truth-about-soft-skills/

[33]   Klaus, P. 2008. *The Hard Truth about Soft Skills: Workplace Lessons Smart People Wish They'd Learned Sooner.* Harper Business. https://amazon.com/Hard-Truth-About-Soft-Skills/dp/0061284149

oral communication, leadership, and adaptability.[34] Looking out across various positions, levels, and industries, Klaus observed "what strikes me most about their stories of missed opportunities and derailed careers is this: The source of their anxiety and frustration invariably stems from a shortcoming in their soft skills repertoire—the nontechnical traits and behaviors needed for successful career navigation."[35]

This eighth principle of committing to employee development is a prudent strategy for the agile manager. Viewing professional development as an integral part of the employee experience can help with employee recruitment, retention, and satisfaction. While 78 percent of employers report providing training or development opportunities to help employees learn new skills but many professionals disagree.[36] Agile managers ensure such a disconnect is far removed from their organization. In one research report, 86 percent of respondents said they would change jobs if it meant more opportunities for professional development.[37] Moreover, LinkedIn's *2018 Workplace Learning Report* found that 94 percent of employees would stay with a company longer if it invested in their career.[38] Two years later, in its *Global Talent Trends 2020* report, LinkedIn reiterated the connection between professional development opportunities and employee recruitment, retention, and satisfaction. "As we enter the 2020s, empathy will reshape the way employers hire and retain talent," said Mark Lobosco, vice president of talent solutions at LinkedIn. A company's purpose, once solely shareholder value, now includes investing in employees. "Companies are becoming more empathetic," Lobosco wrote, "not only to attract candidates, but also to

---

[34] American Management Association, "The Hard Truth About Soft Skills." January 24, 2019. https://amanet.org/articles/the-hard-truth-about-soft-skills/

[35] Klaus, P. 2008. *The Hard Truth about Soft Skills: Workplace Lessons Smart People Wish They'd Learned Sooner.* Harper Business. https:/ amazon.com/Hard-Truth-About-Soft-Skills/dp/0061284149

[36] Fleischman, E. 2019. "Why Employers Need to Invest in Professional Development in 2019." *Forbes*, May 9, 2019. https://tinyurl.com/yctxvbll

[37] Fleischman, E. 2019. "Why Employers Need to Invest in Professional Development in 2019." *Forbes*, May 9, 2019. https://tinyurl.com/yctxvbll

[38] Fleischman, E. 2019. "Why Employers Need to Invest in Professional Development in 2019." *Forbes*, May 9, 2019. https://tinyurl.com/yctxvbll

retain their workforce amid increasing expectations of what employers owe to their people."[39]

Today's VUCA global marketplace presents new challenges to humanity daily. The agile manager will need to leverage compassion as an effective tool in arsenal. Doing so will constantly remind them of the simple fact that managers manage people. Support people in their journey. Help them along their path. And remind them of the opportunities to grow both professionally and personally. Since professional development is linked to personal growth, each manager has the opportunity to support "people through their crises and challenges and help them grow toward becoming their best selves throughout that journey."[40] Today's dynamic, hypercompetitive, and ever changing global marketplace demands a management style that encourages an agile work environment fostering autonomous decision making, work product iteration, experimentation, peer-to-peer coaching, and flexible team structures. As IBM noted in its report *The Enterprise Guide to Closing the Skills Gap* "cultures and organizational competencies need to shift to reflect these new ways of working and facilitate the training and conditioning of a workforce with new skills."[41] Such collaboration and skill development prepares the organization to as the agile manager nurtures relationships with external stakeholders (Principle #9).

Principle #9: Nurture Relationships

The final principle of the agile manager as conductor function involves nurturing relationships with external stakeholders (Principle #9). Customers, partner organizations, and industry related associations are three of the most common types of external stakeholders. Today's VUCA global

---

[39] Maurer, R. 2020. "These 3 Talent Trends for 2020 Focus on Empathy." *LinkedIn*, January 31, 2020. https://shrm.org/resourcesandtools/hr-topics/talent-acquisition/pages/shrm-talent-trends-2020-empathy-employee-experience.aspx

[40] Hassell, D. 2020. "The Real Key to Talent Development is Authentic Caring." *Human Resources Today*, February 13, 2020. https://tinyurl.com/twxckmb

[41] IBM. "The Enterprise Guide to Closing the Skills Gap." 2019. https://ibm.com/downloads/cas/EPYMNBJA

marketplace has created what Alia Crocker and her colleagues defined as "a business environment in which agile collaboration is more critical than ever."[42] Agile collaboration offers the manager in a volatile world the opportunity to expand their mental model beyond the traditional and frequent notion of networking. Many managers, business owners, and executives will proclaim the benefits of networking. For example, Adam Small, CEO of the Strategic Business Network, emphasized the importance of networking by describing it as the "single most powerful tactic to accelerate and sustain success for any individual or organization."[43] To help their organization reach the level of agility required to achieve and sustain growth in a volatile world, however, managers need to understand the relationship between collaborating and networking.

Nurturing relationships through collaboration requires an interactive, purposeful, and balanced approach between organizations. Networking, on the other hand, occurs at the individual level and requires one to remain open minded, identify common interests with others, and maintain an understanding of a diverse group of people. While networking may indeed be "a powerful tactic to accelerate success" at the individual level, the nurturing of relationships with external stakeholders and organizations is a powerful tactic at the organizational level. Networking itself creates individual relationships—people knowing other people. Creating, maintaining, and expanding a network creates the broad and varied foundation required to collaborate. By itself networking seldom create values or collaboration. For example, a LinkedIn profile of over 1,200 connections may illustrate networking prowess but what value has any of those individual level networks generated? Engagement with others for a positive-sum outcome, however, demonstrates the nurturing relationships with external stakeholders so required of the agile manager. As Jim Clifton and Sangeeta Badal wrote in *Born to Build*, "research indicates

[42] Crocker, A., R. Cross, and H.K. Gardner. 2018. "How to Make Sure Agile Teams Can Work Together." *Harvard Business Review*, May 15, 2018. https://hbr.org/2018/05/how-to-make-sure-agile-teams-can-work-together

[43] O'Shea, T. 2014. "How to Network within the Pharmacy World." *Pharmacy Times*, November 24, 2014. https://pharmacytimes.com/contributor/timothy-o-shea/2014/11/how-to-network-within-the-pharmacy-world

successful builders rely on their social networks, cocreate with their customers, and build alliances with their suppliers and investors to reduce uncertainty."[44]

In its 2017 report *Purposeful Collaboration: The Essential Components of Collaborative Cultures*, the Institute for Corporate Productivity (ICP) concluded: "High performing organizations are 2.5 times more likely to encourage interaction with external stakeholders such as clients, suppliers, regulatory bodies, or professional associations."[45] Highlighting the value of nurturing relationships in a volatile world, the ICP recommended senior managers to "require employees who are well-connected internally to work on external connections, or suggest that those who are well-connected externally mentor junior employees in networking to ensure boundary spanning."[46] Such a realization has existed for decades due to the efforts of J. Richard Hackman, a pioneer in the field of organizational behavior. For Hackman, successful collaboration required five essential characteristics that enhanced the likelihood of success: a stable team, a clear and engaging direction, an enabling team structure, a supportive organizational context, and the availability of competent coaching.[47]

To help agile managers create, build, and enhance nurturing and collaborative relationships with external stakeholders and organizations, this principle provides a questionnaire for each team member to complete. Comparing answers between managers and team member can provide some much-needed light on the symmetry, or asymmetry, present within the organization. Identify the gap analysis between the manager and

---

[44] Clifton, J., and S. Badal. 2018. *Born to Build: How to Build a Thriving Startup, A Winning Team, New Customers and Your Best Life Imaginable*. Gallup. https://amazon.com/dp/159562127X/ref=rdr_ext_sb_ti_hist_1

[45] The Institute for Corporate Productivity. 2017. *Purposeful Collaboration: The Essential Components of Collaborative Cultures*. file:///C:/Users/micha/OneDrive/Desktop/Purposeful_Collaboration_i4cp_2017(1).pdf

[46] The Institute for Corporate Productivity. 2017. *Purposeful Collaboration: The Essential Components of Collaborative Cultures*. file:///C:/Users/micha/OneDrive/Desktop/Purposeful_Collaboration_i4cp_2017(1).pdf

[47] Hackman, J.R. 2002. *Leading Teams: Setting the Stage for Great Performances*. Harvard Business School. https://amazon.com/Leading-Teams-Setting-Stage-Performances/dp/1578513332#reader_1578513332

employees as it relates to nurturing relationships with external stakeholders serves as a valuable tool for the organization looking to sustain growth in a volatile world.

1. Do all members of the organization understand the definition of collaboration? This understanding is based on recognizing the difference between networking and collaboration? One of the most common mistakes in any organization is using language without first agreeing upon its definition. As Dean Carter of Pataogoni recognized, "The more a group understands their purpose—why they're coming together, what they're doing to collaborate on a business issue, the better the outcome."[48]

2. Are the organization's goals clear for everyone to understand? Without a clear understanding of the organization's goals, it will be difficult, if not impossible, to identify potential collaboration partners. Such partnerships are an absolute necessity for what Amy Blankson identified as the valuable currency of the future—collaboration.[49]

3. Are the criteria for selecting collaborative partnerships developed, revised, and finalized by members of the team? Micromanaging the decision-making process around the criteria will slow down or prevent the organization from identifying the reasons it needs to pursue external collaborative partnerships.

4. Has the organization aligned collaborative efforts with its goals? It is indeed necessary to (a) define collaboration, (b) have clear goals, and (c) identify collaboration criteria, but if the alignment between the goals and collaborative partnerships remains unclear the nurturing of relationships will be awkward at best and disastrous at worst.

5. Does the organization view collaboration as a critical component of achieving and sustaining growth? Nurturing collaborative relationships

---

[48] The Institute for Corporate Productivity. 2017. *Purposeful Collaboration: The Essential Components of Collaborative Cultures.* file:///C:/Users/micha/OneDrive/Desktop/Purposeful_Collaboration_i4cp_2017(1).pdf

[49] Blankson, A. 2019. "Why Collaboration is the Currency of the Future." *Forbes*, August 15, 2019. https://forbes.com/sites/amyblankson/2019/08/15/why-collaboration-is-the-currency-of-the-future/#908854945e8d

only work if both parties view their work as essential. Nurturing relationships with external stakeholders has always been challenging. While technology has helped facilitate such relationships on one hand, it has also added levels of complexity to the fabric of work. The volatility of today will continue so the agile manager should be ever vigilant in "taking a systematic approach to analyzing how the team is set up to succeed and identifying where improvements are needed since doing so can make all the difference."[50]

6. Are the lines of communication open, clear, and free of judgment? A collaborative venture must create an environment where individuals have the freedom to engage in a productive dialogue without retribution from a manager who needs to control every spoke of the collaborative wheel.

7. When selecting the team members involved for the project, are employees chosen because they have the required skill set for the project or because of their relationship with the manager? The right team members can leverage the relationship to "up-source their knowledge networks, iterate faster, and even expand their use cases for their products."[51]

8. Are roles clearly defined with the work process of a collaboration project between managers and employees? A lack of understanding as to who is doing what will only delay the much-needed progress of a collaborative project. This disorganization of assigned tasks also demonstrates a lack of sophistication when it comes to nurturing relationships. Remember, "taking a partnership-first mindset requires a business to re-examine and potentially disrupt its traditional practices and old ways of operating."[52] As such, people will

---

[50] Haas, M., and M. Mortensen. 2016. "The Secrets of Great Teamwork." *Harvard Business Review*, June 2016. https://hbr.org/2016/06/the-secrets-of-great-teamwork

[51] Blankson, A. 2019. "Why Collaboration is the Currency of the Future." *Forbes*, August 15, 2019. https://forbes.com/sites/amyblankson/2019/08/15/why-collaboration-is-the-currency-of-the-future/#908854945e8d

[52] Auerbach, J. 2018. "Why Partnership is the Business Trend to Watch." *World Economic Forum*, January 16, 2018. https://weforum.org/agenda/2018/01/why-partnership-is-the-business-trend-to-watch/

most likely need to change not only what they are thinking but how they are doing so.

9. What is the process for identify, reporting, and resolving issues that arise during the collaboration project? Team members need a clear path to follow in order to find the answers to questions, solutions to problems, and resolutions to issues that invariably arise during collaboration projects.

10. How is collaboration measured at the employee level? Including collaboration in an employee's performance management will help them identify, assess, and develop this much needed skill essential to the organization's future. In a 19-country global study, ADP reported a mere 16 percent of workers around the world consider themselves "fully engaged" in their jobs; leaving a massive 84 percent of employees defining themselves as simply "just coming to work."[53] The agile manager needs to leverage collaboration opportunities to drive employee engagement and better prepare the organization to meet the dynamics of a volatile world.

In a volatile world, agile managers "need to be continually on the look-out for new market developments and competitive threats, identifying essential experts and nimbly forming and disbanding teams to help tackle those issues quickly." [54] By steadily nurturing agile collaboration, senior management can better utilize the necessary depth of expertise of key collaborators within the organization.[55] Rearranging employees and leveraging their human capital to help the organization achieve a higher level of agility, however, requires the manager to constantly view her employees as

---

[53] "ADP Research Institute Sets International Benchmark for Employee Engagement with its 19-Country Global Study of Engagement," June 14, 2019. www.mediacenter.adp.com/news-releases/news-release-details/adp-research-institute-sets-international-benchmark-employee

[54] Crocker, A., R. Cross, and H.K. Gardner. 2018. "How to Make Sure Agile Teams can Work Together." *Harvard Business Review*, May 15, 2018. https://hbr.org/2018/05/how-to-make-sure-agile-teams-can-work-together

[55] Crocker, A., R. Cross, and H.K. Gardner. 2018. "How to Make Sure Agile Teams can Work Together." *Harvard Business Review*, May 15, 2018. https://hbr.org/2018/05/how-to-make-sure-agile-teams-can-work-together

humans first and workers second. Managing the human capital assigned as collaborative team players can help organizations increase its agility. Although agile collaboration requires a continual reassessment of complex problems, it is possible for firms to combine and recombine essential expertise from across points in the network to address VUCA issues. Doing so embodies the spirit of the fourth function of an agile manager—that of a humanist—who emphasizes the value and agency of human beings, individually and collectively. The human capital needs of today demand managers spend considerable time observing the strengths of each employee (Principle #10). An appreciation of the unique qualities of each person will help the agile manager better understand how to build productive teams (Principle #11). Demonstrating compassion, kindness, and empathy are often understated in the role of management but remain a critical tenet of the agile manager (Principle #12).

Questions

Principle #7: Foster Collaboration

- How would you assess the level of collaboration across your organization?
- What is the organization's track record with collaboration across functional units?
- How often do you work to improve cross-departmental collaboration?
- What could you do as an agile manager to foster collaboration?
- What departments could benefit from increased collaboration?
- Are you aware of the concerns regarding internal collaboration? If so, how can you assuage fears, concerns, and issues?
- What skills, traits, or habits can you leverage to foster collaboration?

Principle #8: Commit to Development

- What have you done recently to demonstrate your own professional development?

- How much time does your organization devote to professional development opportunities for employees?
- When is the last time you helped someone grow professionally or personally?
- How often do you spend on your own professional development?
- What can your organization do to help ignite new professional development training opportunities?
- Do you discuss development opportunities during the interview process for new employees?
- What are some internal barriers to providing new professional development opportunities for employees?
- Have you asked employees recently what training opportunities they would like to see the organization offer?

Principle #9: Nurturing Relationships

- Do all members of the organization understand the definition of collaboration?
- Are the organization's goals clear for everyone to understand?
- Are the criteria for selecting collaborative partnerships developed, revised, and finalized by members of the team?
- Has the organization aligned collaborative efforts with its goals?
- Does the organization view collaboration as a critical component of achieving and sustaining growth?
- Are the lines of communication open, clear, and free of judgment?
- When selecting the team members involved for the project, are employees chosen because they have the required skill set for the project or because of their relationship with the manager?
- Are roles clearly defined with the work process of a collaboration project between managers and employees?
- What is the process for identify, reporting, and resolving issues that arise during the collaboration project?
- How is collaboration measured at the employee level?

CHAPTER 6

Humanist

Introduction to the Fourth Function: Humanist

Years ago, one of my administrative assistants experienced a variety of personal issues that complicated her already difficult like. She felt comfortable explaining an overview of her life situations in case she needed to arrive late some mornings. We had an unwritten agreement that if she arrived late, she would make up the time. She was a model employee and completed her assignments on time. On one Saturday she received a simple text from me that read, "how are you doing?" That is, it. Three words. She responded and thanked me. On the following Monday, she walked into my office and, referring to my text, said, "Boss, thank you for being human." We caught up on the weekend and then went on with our work. Here it is years later and such an exchange has left quite the impression on me. What kind of manager fails to treat their employees as humans? But the bar is so low out there, the professionalism of managers so absent of empathy, and the culture of organizations so void of concern such a simple three-word text meant a world to an administrative assistant. For those managers looking to increase their organization's agility, they should start treating their employees more like humans.

The fourth function of an agile manager is that of a humanist who emphasizes the value and agency of human beings, individually and collectively. The human capital needs of today demand agile managers establish a humanist culture based on diversity, equity, and inclusion (Principle #10). An appreciation of the unique qualities of each person will help the agile manager better understand how to build productive teams (Principle #11). Demonstrating compassion, kindness, and empathy are often understated in the role of management but remain a critical tenet of the agile manager in a volatile world (Principle #12). These three principles form the foundation of the agile manager as a humanist. Such a function remains a priority for managers as today's workplace, and that of tomorrow's, represents unique and ongoing challenges for organizations. One such issue is the high expectations employees have of their employers.

According to a 2018 LinkedIn survey, employees would rather put up with lower pay (65 percent) and forego a fancy title (26 percent) than deal with a bad workplace environment.[1] In other words, a positive and humanist-based organizational culture trumps pay and title for many people. Organizational culture is simply that important. A 2019 white paper by Paychex discussed how today's employees have high expectations of employers. These expectations have disrupted the workplace and will continue to evolve based on advances in technology, generational shifts, and worker preferences.[2] Moreover, in January 2020, prior to the partial shutdown of the U.S. economy as a result of the COVID-19 global pandemic, researchers in another study found only one-third of employees (33 percent) planned to stay at their jobs in 2020, compared to 47 percent who said the same in 2019.[3] Why do employees want to leave their place of work? Disengagement is frequently mentioned as the motivating factor in research, but the underlying cause of disengagement is often a lack of humanist demonstrated by the manager with only 23 percent of employees surveyed stating senior leaders are "very committed" to improving the organizational culture.[4] As such, the tenth principle of the

---

[1] McQueen, N. 2018. "Workplace Culture Trends: The Key to hiring (and keeping) Top Talent in 2018," *LinkedIn,* June 26, 2018. https://blog.linkedin.com/2018/june/26/workplace-culture-trends-the-key-to-hiring-and-keeping-top-talent

[2] "The Future of Work: How Shifting Dynamics, Technological Advances, and Worker Preferences are Disrupting the Workplace of Today." *Paychex,* White Paper.   https://paychex.com/secure/whitepapers/generational-shifts-technology-disrupting-workplace?utm_source=the-hill&utm_medium=press%20release&utm_campaign=future-of-work-277068&utm_term=research

[3] McQueen, N. 2018. "Workplace Culture Trends: The Key to hiring (and keeping) Top Talent in 2018," *LinkedIn,* June 26, 2018. https://blog.linkedin.com/2018/june/26/workplace-culture-trends-the-key-to-hiring-and-keeping-top-talent

[4] McQueen, N. 2018. "Workplace Culture Trends: The Key to hiring (and keeping) Top Talent in 2018," *LinkedIn,* June 26, 2018. https://blog.linkedin.

agile manager in a volatile world is the establishment of an organizational culture built upon humanism.

Principle #10: Establish Culture

To achieve and sustain growth in a volatile world, the agile manager needs to understand just how critical organizational culture is. According to a 2012 survey by Deloitte, "94% of executives and 88% of employees believe a distinct corporate culture is important to a business' success" and noted "exceptional organizations create and sustain a culture that engages and motivates their employees." [5] Additionally, research conducted by CultureIQ uncovered employee's overall ratings of their company's qualities—including collaboration, environment, and values—are rated 20 percent higher in companies that exhibit strong culture.[6] In another survey of over 1,300 senior executives across North American firms, more than half of respondents believed organizational culture is a top-three driver of firm value and 92 percent reported improving their culture would increase their firm's value.[7] Despite the acknowledgment, value, and contribution to an organization's success, only 16 percent of executives and managers reported being satisfied with their culture.[8]

When the low employee engagement statistics are juxtaposed to the dissatisfaction expressed by executives, why are organizational cultures still lacking? The short answer is because managers lack the agility required

---

com/2018/june/26/workplace-culture-trends-the-key-to-hiring-and-keeping-top-talent

[5] Deloitte. 2012. "Core Beliefs and Culture: Chairman's Survey Findings." https://www2.deloitte.com/content/dam/Deloitte/global/Documents/About-Deloitte/gx-core-beliefs-and-culture.pdf

[6] The 2017 TCC report: Building a high-performance culture: key lessons from top cultures, Culture IQ, https://go.pardot.com/l/455712/2017-11-23/d2qyhn

[7] Graham, J.R., et. al. 2017. "Corporate Culture: Evidence from the Field." National Business Economic Research Working Paper No. 23255, March 2017. https://nber.org/papers/w23255

[8] Graham, J.R., et. al. 2017. "Corporate Culture: Evidence from the Field." National Business Economic Research Working Paper No. 23255, March 2017. https://nber.org/papers/w23255

to create a humanist-based organizational culture. Everyone seems aware of the problem but choose to ignore it. The agile manager does not have that luxury. In 2020 and beyond, the agile manager operating in a volatile world who creates a humanist-based organizational culture needs to have a commitment to the three hallmarks of the workplace of today and tomorrow: diversity, inclusion, and equity (DEI). Managing in a VUCA environment requires a culture where each member can thrive, grow, and align their work with the short-term and long-term sustainability of the organization. While the literature on DEI initiatives continues to grow, here are working definitions managers can start with as they look to create a humanist-based organizational culture.

- *Diversity* encompasses the various characteristics involved with making one individual or group different from another. Often refers to race, ethnicity, and gender, diversity can also include age, national origin, religion, disability, sexual orientation, socioeconomic status, education, marital status, language, and physical appearance. Some definitions can also include diversity of ideas, perspectives, and values.[9]
  - *Question for the agile manager*: Is your organizational culture committed to diversity? If so, how do you know and what is your working definition of diversity for your organization?
- *Equity* involves creating a culture of fairness, access, and opportunity while simultaneously striving to identify and eliminate barriers that have prevented the full participation of some groups. A culture involving equity helps to improve fairness within the procedures and processes of organizations as well as the distribution of resources.[10]

---

[9] Kapila, M., E. Hines, and M. Searby. 2016. "ProInspire, Why Diversity, Equity, and Inclusion Matter, Independent Sector." October 6, 2016. https://independentsector.org/resource/why-diversity-equity-and-inclusion-matter/

[10] Kapila, M., E. Hines, and M. Searby. 2016. "ProInspire, Why Diversity, Equity, and Inclusion Matter, Independent Sector." October 6, 2016. https://independentsector.org/resource/why-diversity-equity-and-inclusion-matter/

- ○ *Question for the agile manager:* What has your organization done lately to improve fairness, access, and opportunity for all persons?
- *Inclusion* requires an environment to make anyone feel welcomed, respected, supported, and valued. Such inclusion is a prerequisite for individuals to participate in, and have a positive experience with, the organizational culture.[11]
  - ○ *Question for the agile manager:* How has your organization updated its culture to reflect a more inclusive environment where everyone feels welcomed, respected, supported and valued?

The relevance of diversity, equity, and inclusion as drivers of a humanist-based organizational culture today continues to grow. As Deborah S. Willis noted, "there is a rapidly growing movement among employers to require job applicants to demonstrate both commitment and contributions to diversity."[12] Formally known as DEI aptitude (diversity, equity and inclusion) employers are now asking DEI-related questions in the interview process.[13] As an illustration that DEI aptitude has taken its place in the forefront of national conversations and policy, new executive leadership positions overseeing DEI efforts in corporations, government agencies, schools, and nonprofit organizations continue to emerge.

Cultivating a humanist-based organizational culture based on DEI initiatives is simply good for business. The agile manager should take note of Rebekah Bastian's observation: "The importance of Diversity, Equity and Inclusion (DEI) initiatives as a part of an employee engagement

[11] Kapila, M., E. Hines, and M. Searby. 2016. "ProInspire, Why Diversity, Equity, and Inclusion Matter, Independent Sector." October 6, 2016. https://independentsector.org/resource/why-diversity-equity-and-inclusion-matter/
[12] Willis, D.S. 2017. "Getting Up to Speed on Diversity." *Inside Higher Ed,* August 21, 2017. https://insidehighered.com/advice/2017/08/21/how-graduate-students-can-demonstrate-commitment-diversity-job-interviews-essay
[13] Willis, D.S. 2017. "Getting Up to Speed on Diversity." *Inside Higher Ed,* August 21, 2017. https://insidehighered.com/advice/2017/08/21/how-graduate-students-can-demonstrate-commitment-diversity-job-interviews-essay

strategy cannot be understated."[14] Creating a humanist-based organizational culture based upon the DEI initiatives will contribute to the changing workforce of today and tomorrow. As new generations enter the workforce, their perspectives, mental models, and values will increasingly challenge the agility of both the manager and organization. Many human resource professionals now report their organizations need an updated organizational culture to meet the expectations of new generations in the workforce. Only those organizations nimble enough to adapt will survive.[15] To adapt and embrace the fluid workplace, the agile manager who has created a DEI-based organizational culture (Principle #10) can then begin to appreciate the unique qualities of each person to build productive teams (Principle #11).

Principle #11: Appreciate Uniqueness

As discussed in Principle #10, "culture drives everything that happens in an organization, good or bad."[16] Once the agile manager creates a culture based on diversity, equity, and inclusion (Principle #10), the next humanist function would be an appreciation of the unique qualities of each person (Principle #11). To appreciate employees, one must first understand that many leaders fail to pay enough attention to the behaviors, needs, and troubles of employees.[17] This ignorance, intentional or not, needs to stop if an organization hopes to survive in a volatile world. Acknowledging employees as humans and exercising a curiosity about

---

[14] Bastian, R. 2019. "Corporate DEI Initiatives are Good for Everyone: Including You." *Forbes*, February 25, 2019. https://forbes.com/sites/rebekah-bastian/2019/02/25/corporate-dei-initiatives-are-good-for-everyone-including-you/#6b2eeb6966c3

[15] "HR agility: Embracing the Fluid Workforce." *Ultimate Software and Forrester Research*, April 2020, https://ultimatesoftware.com/ContactForm/7010d000001Kzx4

[16] Hogan, M. 2016. "Seven Qualities that Make Great Managers So Effective." *Forbes*, January 26, 2016. https://forbes.com/sites/yec/2016/01/26/seven-qualities-the-best-managers-share-and-why-they-matter/#4833edb83d74

[17] Sutton, R.I. 2018. "How Bosses Waste their Employees' Time." *The Wall Street Journal*, August 12, 2018. https://dontwait.wsj.com/2018/Waste-Time.html

them is a by-product of emotional intelligence, often known as emotional quotient (EQ). As Travis Bradberry wrote in *Emotional Intelligence 2.0* published in 2009, "research now points to emotional intelligence as being the critical factor that sets star performers apart from the rest of the pack. The connection is so strong that 90% of top performers have high emotional intelligence."[18] For decades, researchers believed intelligence quotient (IQ) to be the driving factor behind success. Subsequent studies discovered, however, that people with average IQs outperform those with the highest IQs 70 percent of the time.[19]

Improving self-awareness as an agile manager allows one to create a ripple effect creating a higher level of emotional intelligence.[20] By understanding one's strengths and weaknesses, the agile manager can more accurately assess their emotional intelligence, that, in turn, can help them appreciate the uniqueness of each employee.[21] Appreciating the unique qualities of each employee or team member illustrates a curiosity about others, which is a by-product of empathy. The more empathetic the agile manager the more employees are treated as humans. This self-awareness, appreciation of uniqueness, and empathy allows the agile manager the opportunity to create a humanistic-based culture where employees are a high degree autonomy. This autonomy, much like the humanistic-based culture and agile environment itself is a means, not an end. As Steve Denning wrote in *Forbes*, "the goal is to enable the organization to generate instant, frictionless, intimate, incremental, risk-free value at scale" to

---

[18] Bradberry, T. 2019. "14 Signs that you are Incredibly Emotionally Intelligent— and a High Performer." *LinkedIn*, October 31, 2019. https://businessinsider.com/ high-performers-emotionally-intelligent-signs-2019-4

[19] Bradberry, T. 2019. "14 Signs that you are Incredibly Emotionally Intelligent— and a High Performer." *LinkedIn*, October 31, 2019. https://businessinsider.com/ high-performers-emotionally-intelligent-signs-2019-4

[20] Crompton, M. 2010. "Improving Self-Awareness Increases your Emotional Intelligence." *Peoria*, April 2010. https://peoriamagazines.com/ibi/2010/apr/ improving-self-awareness-increases-your-emotional-intelligence

[21] "The Importance of Emotional Intelligence to the CFO Role: Pete Shimer, CFO, Deloitte." *The Wall Street Journal*, January 12, 2018. https://deloitte.wsj .com/riskandcompliance/2018/01/12/the-importance-of-emotional- intelligence-to-the-cfo-role-pete-shimer-cfo-deloitte/

achieve short-term and long-term sustainability.[22] Reminding employees of the difference between the means and the end can be a useful tool in the agile manager's armamentarium. Such a tool becomes even more valuable in an organizational culture fostering autonomy for employees.

The evidence overwhelmingly demonstrates the value of a culture operating on a high degree of autonomy, often defined as when employees have a choice in how to achieve their day-to-day work. The research convincingly shows how autonomy is a key attribute of job satisfaction and leads to higher retention rates and greater productivity. "Robert Burgelman and Joseph Bower have shown a relationship between autonomy (of both individuals and units) and the growth of innovative ideas and ventures within companies."[23] Daniel Wheatley provided further evidence of the value of autonomy and observed "greater levels of control over work tasks and schedule have the potential to generate significant benefits for the employee."[24] Autonomy is such a strong indicator of employee satisfaction the results of one study involving more than 2,000 people across three continents consistently found that, although employees without a lot of power do indeed desire more of it, ultimately "gaining autonomy quenches the desire for power."[25] In other words, autonomy trumps power.

Conversely, the research also indicates the consequences of an organizational culture failing to offer employees autonomy. Researchers have found stress, dissatisfaction, malaise, and a feeling of being micromanaged

[22] Denning, S. 2018. "The 12 stages of the Agile Transformation Journey." *Forbes*, November 4, 2018. https://forbes.com/sites/stevedenning/2018/11/04/the-twelve-stages-of-the-agile-transformation-journey/#77ab9db13dd4

[23] Gulati, R. 2018. "Structure that's Not Stifling." *Harvard Business Review*, May–June 2018. https://hbr.org/2018/05/structure-thats-not-stifling

[24] Wheatley, D. 2017. "Autonomy in Paid Work and Employee Subjective Well-Being." *Work and Occupations* 44, no, 3. https://journals.sagepub.com/doi/10.1177/0730888417697232

[25] Lammers, J., et. al. 2016. "To Have Control Over or to be Free from Others? The Desire for Power Reflects a Need for Autonomy." *Personality and Social Psychology Bulletin* 42, no. 4. https://journals.sagepub.com/doi/abs/10.1177/0146167216634064?rss=1

as consistent with cultures void of autonomy.[26] A study from the Indiana University Kelley School of Business was published in November 2016. The research team examined how stress and levels of control affected over 2,300 employees. "When comparing highly-demanding jobs, those that also gave employees less control were associated with a 15.4 percent increased chance of death."[27] Does the agile manager who needs to achieve sustainable growth really want to have a culture where employees are worked to death? Does the employee want to work in an organizational culture where micromanagement levels are driving people to an early death?

It is imperative, therefore, for today's manager to understand the humanistic function of their position and the contribution of the unique traits of each employee. The agile manager must visualize the type of organizational culture they believe best represents a humanistic approach and then seek to translate that vision into reality. As Deloitte CFO Pete Shimer discussed in a *Wall Street Journal* interview, building a team consisting of individuals that compliment your skills demonstrate both a recognition of their uniqueness and an acknowledgment of the value they bring to the table. According to Shimer, "I build my team with the skillsets that supplement my abilities. Then I rely on their abilities, delegating responsibility and allowing them to do things their way—even if they choose a way that's not my first choice."[28]

Despite the overwhelming evidence for a culture based on an appreciation of uniqueness and autonomy, there remains a gap between what workers value and how the organizational culture operates. While research

---

[26] Bell, A. 2020. "3 Easy and Practical Ways to Achieve Autonomy in the Workplace." *Snacknation*, January 10, 2020. https://snacknation.com/blog/autonomy-in-the-workplace/

[27] Gonzalez-Mulé, E., and B. Cockburn. Spring 2017. "Worked to Death: The Relationships of Job Demands and Job Control with Mortality." *Personnel Psychology* 70, no. 1. https://onlinelibrary.wiley.com/doi/pdf/10.1111/peps.12206

[28] "The Importance of Emotional Intelligence to the CFO Role: Pete Shimer, CFO, Deloitte." *The Wall Street Journal*, January 12, 2018. https://deloitte.wsj.com/riskandcompliance/2018/01/12/the-importance-of-emotional-intelligence-to-the-cfo-role-pete-shimer-cfo-deloitte/

has confirmed this gap at the macro level, the agile manager needs to conduct their own assessment and identify the level of disconnect at the micro level. For example, the 2019 Deloitte study *Global Human Capital Trends* employees ranked "not understanding what's important to employees" as the greatest barrier to changing the company's culture.[29] Lack of funding and lack of leadership support for change came in second and third respectively.[30] The misalignment is also referred to by Robert A Cooke as the "culture disconnect."[31] The agile manager needs to ensure cultural disconnects—when the organizational structure is driven more by current resources rather than by organizational values—are resolved in order to create a humanistic culture based on the appreciation of the unique attributes of each person.

Research has found "leaders seeking to build high-performing organizations are often confounded by culture."[32] For those managers solely focused on the bottom line, they hand-off the development of culture to other departments in the organization such as human resources. But in today's volatile world, leaders can ill afford to remain confounded or hands-off. It is the responsibility of the leader to create a humanistic culture so the organization can implement the level of agility required to sustain both short-term and long-term growth. Since most managers inherit a culture the task before them involves modernizing, improving, and reforming. How they go about updating their culture will ultimately determine how their organization responds to the ongoing volatility. As Boris Groysberg and colleagues noted, "For better and worse, culture

[29] Volini, E., J. Schwartz, and I. Roy. 2019. "2019 Global Human Capital Trends," Deloitte Insights, April 11, 2019. https://www2.deloitte.com/us/en/insights/focus/human-capital-trends/2019/rewards-employees-want-most.html

[30] Volini, E., J. Schwartz, and I. Roy. 2019. "2019 Global Human Capital Trends," Deloitte Insights, April 11, 2019. https://www2.deloitte.com/us/en/insights/focus/human-capital-trends/2019/rewards-employees-want-most.html

[31] Szumal, J.L. "If your organization experiencing a culture disconnect?," https://humansynergistics.com/docs/default-source/research-publications/culture-disconnect.pdf

[32] Groysberg, B., J. Lee, J. Price, and J.Y. Cheng. 2018. "The Leader's Guide to Corporate Culture." *Harvard Business Review,* January–February 2018. https://hbr.org/2018/01/the-culture-factor

and management are inextricably linked with the best leaders aware of the multiple cultures within which they are embedded, can sense when change is required, and can deftly influence the process."[33] Once the agile manager creates a culture based on diversity, equity, and inclusion (Principle #10) and then demonstrates an appreciation of the unique qualities of each person (Principle #11), the third principle within this function would be to show compassion, kindness, and empathy to employees (Principle #12).

Principle #12: Demonstrate Compassion

Once the agile manager creates a culture based on diversity, equity, and inclusion (Principle #10) and then demonstrates an appreciation of the unique qualities of each person (Principle #11), the third principle within this humanistic function would be to show compassion, kindness, and empathy to employees (Principle #12). In today's volatile world, it is more important than ever for leaders to figure out how to create a humanistic culture based on compassion so their organization can compete in today's hypercompetitive global marketplace.[34] In his best-selling 1989 book *Leadership Is an Art*, former Herman Miller CEO Max De Pree proclaimed, "The first responsibility of a leader is to define reality. The last is to say thank you. In between the two, the leader must become a servant."[35] How the agile manager communicates the reality of the challenges, issues, and concerns facing the organization is just as important as the explanation itself. One needs to exercise compassion when discussing the dynamics of today's volatile global marketplace. According to the *2020 State of Workplace Empathy Study*, much work remains here

---

[33] Groysberg, B., J. Lee, J. Price, and J. Yo-Jud Cheng. 2018. "The Leader's Guide to Corporate Culture." *Harvard Business Review*, January–February 2018. https://hbr.org/2018/01/the-culture-factor

[34] 2020 State of Workplace Empathy, business solver https://businessolver.com/resources/state-of-workplace-empathy

[35] DePree, M. 1989. *Leadership is An Art*. Random House. https://amazon.com/Leadership-Art-Max-Depree/dp/0385264968/ref=tmm_hrd_swatch_0?_encoding=UTF8&qid=&sr=#reader_0385264968

as 72 percent of CEOs surveyed said empathy needs to improve.[36] Like the other management principles for a volatile world discussed throughout this publication, ample research supports the value of demonstrating compassion for the agile manager.

In their examination into compassionate leadership, Charmi Patel and Kiran Kandade found 70 percent of respondents who experienced compassion from their leaders were more productive than those that did not.[37] Gallup's meta-analysis of decades' worth of data published in 2016 shows employees having a strong connection with one's work and colleagues, feeling like a real contributor, and enjoying ample chances to learn—consistently leads to higher productivity, better-quality products, and increased profitability.[38] Paul J. Zak and his research team discovered that "employees in high-trust organizations are more productive, have more energy at work, collaborate better with their colleagues, and are happier with their lives; all of these factors fuel stronger organizational performance."[39] "Being benevolent is important because it can change the perception your followers have of you," said Chou-Yu Tsai, an assistant professor of management at Binghamton University's School of Management. "If you feel that your leader or boss actually cares about you, you may feel more serious about the work you do for them."[40] Examples from companies across a spectrum of industries illustrate compassionate management practices.

---

[36] 2020 State of Workplace Empathy, Business Solver. https://businessolver.com/resources/state-of-workplace-empathy

[37] Laker, B. 2020. "How to be More Compassionate During Coronavirus Crisis." *Forbes*, April 14, 2020. https://forbes.com/sites/benjaminlaker/2020/04/14/how-to-be-more-compassionate-during-covid-19-crisis/#1c63f8b9574d

[38] Harter, J. 2016. "Moneyball for Business: Employee Engagement Meta-Analysis." *Gallup*, May 31, 2016. https://gallup.com/workplace/236468/moneyball-business-employee-engagement-meta-analysis.aspx?g_source=EMPLOYEE_ENGAGEMENT&g_medium=topic&g_campaign_tiles

[39] Zak, P.J. 2017. "The Neuroscience of Trust." *Harvard Business Review*, January–February 2017. https://hbr.org/2017/01/the-neuroscience-of-trust

[40] Binghamton University. "It pays to be Nice to your Employees: Showing Discipline with Kindness, Compassion to Employees Results in Better Job Performance." *ScienceDaily*. www.sciencedaily.com/releases/2018/09/180911132049.htm

The tech industry, for example, an area that routinely struggles to employ enough women, has progressed in terms of parental leave. HP offers a minimum of 10 and a maximum of 16 weeks paid time off for new moms while Airbnb gives birth mothers 22 paid weeks of maternity leave, while nonbirth parents get 10 weeks.[41] Netflix, however, offers the longest paid family leave out of all the tech companies. In 2015, Netflix employees were given 52 weeks of paid parental leave as part of their employment package. This benefit, which applies to both parents, gives employees the flexibility to come back to work and resume leave as it suits them. Netflix based these policy updates on the research that happy employees are healthier, more motivated, and less likely to leave the team for employment elsewhere.[42]

Celgene offers another example of compassionate management. In 2019, the global biopharmaceutical company was recognized as the Best Place to Work for LGBTQ Equality and achieved a Corporate Equality Index (CEI) of 100 percent for 2019. The CEI is a national benchmarking tool on corporate policies and practices relating to lesbian, gay, bisexual, transgender and queer employees (LGBTQ). Administered by the Human Rights Campaign Foundation, an annual CEI survey is sent to hundreds of global companies to evaluate an array of LGBTQ-related policies and practices. Celgene's perfect CEI rating reflects initiatives such as the Celgene Pride Alliance, which includes mentorship, volunteering, and employee inclusion groups for LGBTQ employees and allies. Like Netflix's updated parental leave policy, Celgene's compassionate management practices promote employee development, retention, and foster an inclusive workplace where colleagues are recognized and respected as their authentic selves. "The main goal for our growing list of employee resource groups is to promote employee development and learning, drive

---

[41] Moila, R. 2018. "Netflix Parents Get a Paid Year Off and Amazon Pays for Spouses' Parental Leave." *Vox*, January 31, 2018. https://vox.com/2018/1/31/16944976/new-parents-tech-companies-google-hp-facebook-twitter-netflix

[42] "Examining Corporate Social Responsibility in the Industrial Space." *Thomas Net*, September 23, 2019. https://thomasnet.com/insights/corporate-social-responsibility-examples/

engagement and model inclusive behavior where all colleagues can be their authentic selves at work," said Juli Blanche, VP, Talent Acquisition & Employee Experience. "Inclusivity and diversity in the workplace not only create a more welcoming environment—it fosters new ideas, approaches and innovation across our entire business."[43]

During the COVID-19 global pandemic during 2020, many companies updated policies, revised programs, and donated services and money to demonstrate high levels of compassion. Proctor & Gamble shifted production at Gillette intended for razors, rendered less essential by remote working, and to face shields being donated to local hospitals.[44] The French luxury conglomerate LVMH converted its assembly lines of expensive perfume for hand sanitizer that it donated to the French government.[45] Starbucks provided a number of compassionate initiatives including giving employees the option to stay home with pay through May 3, even if their location was open, offering an additional $3/hour for employees who chose to work their shifts, and expanding its mental health benefits for employees who work more than 20 hours a week at no cost.[46] In an open letter dated April 16, 2020 and published on its website Rossann Williams, EVP and president, wrote to Starbucks employees: "We know this is an unprecedented time, and we want every partner to know you have options when it comes to doing what is best for you. Whatever you

---

[43] "The Human Rights Campaign Foundation Names Celgene Best Place to Work for LGBTQ Equality for 2019." March 28, 2019. https://celgene.com/celgene-named-best-place-to-work-for-lgbtq-equality-2019/

[44] Chesto, J. 2020. "P&G is Making Tens of Thousands of Face Shields at Gillette Plant in Southie." *Boston Globe,* April 13, 2020. https://bostonglobe.com/2020/04/13/business/pg-is-making-tens-thousands-face-shields-gillette-plant-southie/

[45] Samaha, B. 2020. "The Fashion and Beauty Companies Helping to Combat the Effects of Coronavirus." *Harper's Bazaar,* April 27, 2020. https://harpersbazaar.com/fashion/designers/a31901094/fashion-beauty-companies-coronavirus-donation/

[46] "Navigating through COVID-19." *Starbucks Website.* https://stories.starbucks.com/stories/2020/navigating-through-covid-19/

choose, I want you to know that your Starbucks family stands with you, today and always. We will always have your back."[47]

According to Leah Weiss, PhD, author of *How We Work: Live Your Purpose, Reclaim Your Sanity, and Embrace the Daily Grind*, "*The costs of an organization where people are not deeply committed [to compassion] far outweigh what the investment would have been to help.*"[48] *To achieve the level of agility required of an organization to sustain both short-term and long-term growth in today's volatile, uncertain, complex, and ambiguous global marketplace, agile managers need to demonstrate compassion. Doing so allows them to practice the humanistic function of management and create a culture where people feel a genuine connection and want to support the mission, goals, and vision of the organization. With a positive organizational culture in place, one can then turn their attention toward the fifth function of the agile manager: that of an advocate promoting the work, employees, and value of the organization.*

Questions

Principle #10: Establishing Culture

- How often do you think about culture as a critical force to leverage to create a more agile organization?
- Have you thought about the relationship between agility and culture?
- How would you describe your organization's culture currently?
- Have you surveyed your employee's attitude toward organizational culture?

---

[47] Williams, R. 2020. "A Letter to Partners: Comprehensive Partner Care as We Adapt to COVID-19." *Starbucks Website*, April 16, 2020. https://stories. starbucks.com/stories/2020/a-letter-to-partners-comprehensive-partner-care-as-we-adapt-to-covid-19/

[48] Dube, R. 2019. "How Kindness & Compassion can Reduce Company Turnover." *Forbes*, December 9, 2019. https://forbes.com/sites/robdube/2019/ 12/09/how-kindness--compassion-can-reduce-company-turnover/#12355d 972845

- What have you done lately to improve the organizational culture?
- Do you clearly understand your role in creating the organizational culture?
- Have you explained to everyone their role in fostering a positive organizational culture?
- What are some barriers, perceived and real, to improving the organizational culture?
- Can everyone clearly articulate your organization's approach to diversity, equity, and inclusion?

Principle #11: Appreciate Uniqueness

- How much time do you spend thinking about the unique traits of each employee?
- Have you assessed your emotional intelligence (EQ)?
- What have you done lately to demonstrate an appreciation of uniqueness among employees?
- Have you asked employees to describe what is important to them in terms of culture?
- What is your view of the organizational culture?
- Have you thought about the relationship between agility and the unique traits of each employee?
- Where do you see areas of improvement in the organizational culture? Is that in alignment with what the employees recorded?

Principle #12: Demonstrate Compassion

- Would you consider the demonstration of compassion a weakness? Why? Why not?
- What is the relationship between your organization's culture and compassion?
- How would you describe your level of compassion toward your employees?

- What have you done lately to demonstrate compassion toward others?
- Have you witnessed employees being compassionate toward one another?
- Where do you think some additional compassion could benefit your organizational culture?
- Do you have difficulty demonstrating compassion? Explain.
- What are some internal barriers to demonstrating additional compassion?

CHAPTER 7

Advocate

Introduction to Function #5: Advocate

The fifth function of an agile manager is that of an advocate promoting the work, employees, and value of the organization as it looks to break through the inordinate amount of noise in the volatile global marketplace. Tracing the etymology of the word, "advocate" helps managers better understand this function. The word has its origins in Middle English, from Old French avocat, from Latin *advocatus*, past participle (used as a noun) of advocate "call (to one's aid)," from ad- "to" + vocare "to call." As an advocate, you publicly call for, support, and promote your organization's mission, employees, and partners. To achieve both short-term and long-term growth, agile managers would serve their organizations well by advocating for their employees when dealing with internal stakeholders, clients, and the public. The three principles involved with this function focus on what to do, how to do it, and where to do it. Creating content on a regular basis will help the agile manager promote the work of the organization—*what* to do (Principle #13). Telling stories about the people who work there can help the organization relate to customers, partners, and suppliers—*how* to do it (Principle #14). The manager then needs to diversity the distribution of both the content and stories to as many social media platforms and outlets as possible—*where* to do it (Principle #15).

As Firas Kittaneh, cofounder and CEO of Amerisleep, noted the importance of the managerial function of advocate in a September 2018 *Inc.* article and wrote, "Leaders must learn how to be consistent and effective advocates for their staff in order to cultivate quality relationships that will increase engagement and performance levels."[1] Psychologist and

---

[1] Kittaneh, F. 2018. "3 Ways Leaders Can Become Outstanding Advocates for Their Team." *Inc.*, September 25, 2018. https://inc.com/firas-kittaneh/3-ways-leaders-can-become-outstanding-advocates-for-their-team.html

author Sherrie Campbell defines advocacy as acknowledging the dignity, worth, and value of each employee. "When we acknowledge the dignity and worth of another," Campbell argues, "we are seeing them...for who they are in the world, for what they do, and to tell them why what they do and who they are matters."[2] Within some organizations like American Express, advocacy is embedded into their culture of diversity, equity, and inclusion. "With women comprising nearly 40 percent of our executives and a workforce that is over 50 percent female," Sonia Cargan, chief diversity officer at American Express, noted, "we have seen firsthand the positive change women can collectively drive across the enterprise. As my team looks toward the future, we are focused on encouraging even stronger advocacy to make our workplace more inclusive."[3] Creating content for employees, partners, and customers is a new and effective strategy agile managers can use as they look to advocate for their organizations.

Principle #13: Create Content

As an advocate for their organization in a volatile world, the agile manager needs to understand how the dynamics have shifted leadership from a passive role to that of an activist. The agile manager who creates content serves as an advocate but also as an illustration of how leadership continues to evolve in today's dynamic global marketplace. As hyper-connectedness, disruption, and innovation continue to impact the evolution of the modern business world, leadership must also evolve if an organization is to achieve any level of sustainability. "Leadership has been fundamentally redefined," according to Craig Mullaney, Partner, Brunswick Group, who said, "a modern leader needs to influence, inspire, and inform people with direct, engaging, and authentic digital communications. The old playbook isn't enough."[4]

[2] Campbell, S. 2017. "8 Ways to Advocate for Your Team's Success." *Entrepreneur*, February 23, 2017. https://entrepreneur.com/article/289583

[3] Cargan, S. 2018. "Enabling a Workplace Culture of Ambition and Advocacy." *HR Executive*, July 10, 2018. https://hrexecutive.com/enabling-a-workplace-culture-of-ambition-and-advocacy/

[4] Press Release: Brunswick's Connected Leadership Defines New Expectations for CEOs, Brunswick, June 11, 2019. https://brunswickgroup.com/press-release-brunswick-s-connected-leadership-defines-new-expectations-for-ceos-i11248/

Recent research has uncovered new and important trends for the agile manager operating in a volatile world. To understand leadership in the modern and connected world, the strategic advisory firm Brunswick conducted its Connected Leadership Survey in June 2019 measuring the expectations of CEOs from 4,000 employees and 400 financial readers in the United States and UK. While CEOs are expected to focus on financial and strategic issues, there is now an increasing expectation for direct communication with both the public and investors as the public face of the company. The Connected Leadership Survey results show "a majority of U.S. and UK employees believe that communication on social media from a CEO has a positive impact on the company's overall effectiveness (66% U.S. and UK) and reputation (71% U.S., 72% UK)."[5]

Moreover, the 2019 Edelman Trust Barometer: Expectations for CEOs report found that a majority of people believe CEOs should communicate with the public via social media (63 percent), an even larger majority (79 percent) say knowing a CEO's personal values is important to building trust, and spontaneous speakers are more trusted than those who deliver well-rehearsed speeches.[6] Around 65 percent of U.S. employees say it's important for CEOs to actively communicate about their companies online, particularly during times of crisis, the report found. Additionally, 60 percent of employees say they would check an executive's social media before joining a company.

Even though the evidence overwhelmingly demonstrates the benefits of leaders who advocate for their organization by creating content, for many small business owners and CEOs doing so is often considered an unnecessary distraction. According to one 2019 survey, 40 percent of small business owners do not own a Web site and 28 percent of those believe a Web site is irrelevant for their business.[7] In today's volatile world,

---

[5] Press Release: Brunswick's Connected Leadership Defines New Expectations for CEOs, Brunswick, June 11, 2019. https://brunswickgroup.com/press-release-brunswick-s-connected-leadership-defines-new-expectations-for-ceos-i11248/

[6] The 2019 Edelman Trust Barometer: Expectations for CEOs, April 29, 2019. https://edelman.com/research/trust-barometer-expectations-for-ceos-2019

[7] "More Than One-Third of Small Businesses Have No Website, Survey Finds." Visual Objects Press Release Dated February 28, 2019. https://prnewswire.com/

where 4.57 billion people or 59 percent of the global population are classified as active Internet users, small business owners and leaders need to understand the number of people online will only continue to increase.[8] With the level of Internet usage almost guaranteed to increase for the foreseeable future, it behooves the small business owner to understand "without a digital presence in some way, people who don't know you may not trust your business."[9] Additionally, as of June 2019, over 60 percent of CEOs lacked a social media presence.[10] For the minority of CEOs that do create content, however, they understand the value of doing so and serve as advocates. For example, Walmart CEO Doug McMillon posts to Facebook nearly every day while Nasdaq's chief Adena Friedman regularly engages with her nearly half a million LinkedIn followers.[11] "Social media…provides an unfiltered forum for corporate leaders to listen to their communities and to connect by sharing their successes and challenges," Adena Friedman, president and CEO of Nasdaq, told Brunswick Group "Social media projects the human side of the corporate world."[12]

The notion of leader as advocate through creating content has been around for over a century. Over 120 years ago, John Deere launched perhaps the first advocacy campaign and created content for farmers via *The Furrow*, an agriculture magazine still in circulation today with

---

news-releases/more-than-one-third-of-small-businesses-have-no-website-survey-finds-300803983.html

[8] "Global Digital Population as of April 2020." https://statista.com/statistics/617136/digital-population-worldwide/

[9] "More Than One-Third of Small Businesses Have No Website, Survey Finds." Visual Objects press release dated February 28, 2019. https://prnewswire.com/news-releases/more-than-one-third-of-small-businesses-have-no-website-survey-finds-300803983.html

[10] Tourville, S. 2019. "Why the CEO and C-Suite Should be on Social Media." *PR News*, August 14, 2019. https://prnewsonline.com/CEO-social+media

[11] Akhtar, A. 2019. "4 things the Best CEOs do on Social Media to make Authentic Connections with their Followers." Business Insider, June 11, 2019. https://businessinsider.com/why-and-how-ceos-should-use-social-media-2019-6

[12] Gravier, E. 2019. "The Top 10 Most 'Connected' CEOs on Social Media–and Where You Can Follow Them." *CNBC*, June 25, 2019. https://cnbc.com/2019/06/25/the-10-most-connected-ceos-on-social-media.html

a readership of over 550,000.[13] In some respects *The Furrow's* existence for over 120 years demonstrates how little has changed. But such longevity also signifies the need for content to be created and shared by leaders who serve as advocates for their industry, employees, and clients. As one observer noted, "leaders cannot afford to stay safely tucked away in an ivory tower. They must understand how the different parts of their enterprise work. They must stay on top of developments in other industries. They have to get outside their offices, and talk and listen to their employees, their customers, their stakeholders, their investors and their partners as much as they can."[14] Only then can one truly be an agile manager who functions as an advocate.

The fifth function of an agile manager is that of an advocate promoting the work, employees, and value of the organization as it looks to break through the inordinate amount of noise in the marketplace. The three principles involved with this function focus on what to do, how to do it, and where to do it. Creating content on a regular basis will help the agile manager promote the work of the organization—what to do (Principle #13). Telling stories about the people who work there can help the organization relate to customers, partners, and suppliers—how to do it (Principle #14). The manager then needs to diversity the distribution of both the content and stories to as many social media platforms and outlets as possible—where to do it (Principle #15).

Principle #14: Tell Stories

The agile manager as an advocate (Function #5) creates content (Principle #13) and then tells stories about the people who work there can help the organization relate to customers, partners, and suppliers (Principle #14).

---

[13] Smiley, M. 2018. "John Deere, the 'OG Content Marketer,' on how its 123-year-Old Magazine Endures." *The Drum*, May 24, 2018. https://thedrum.com/news/2018/05/24/john-deere-the-og-content-marketer-how-its-123-year-old-magazine-endures

[14] Stephenson, C. 2011. "How Leadership Has Changed." *Ivey Business Journal*, July/August 2011. https://iveybusinessjournal.com/publication/how-leadership-has-changed/

The role of stories in society has been the subject of much debate over time. Suffice it to say philosophers, social scientists, and other researchers will often refer to two different modes of cognition: the narrative mode and the paradigmatic mode. The narrative mode, also known as the narrative paradigm, is a theory developed by twentieth-century communication scholar Walter Fisher. This paradigm makes two distinct proclamations: first, all meaningful communication occurs via storytelling, and second, stories are more persuasive than arguments. Fisher's narrative paradigm rests in direct contrast to the paradigmatic mode, or rational world paradigm associated with the teachings of Plato and Aristotle. The rational world paradigm suggests an argument is most persuasive when it is logical. While both approaches are useful tools for the agile manager operating in a volatile world, understanding the historical development of storytelling over the centuries provides some much-needed perspective for those attempting to create a more agile organization.

Agile managers operating as advocates in a volatile world should become familiar with two communication concepts: the information exchange rate (IER) and the knowledge production rate (KPR). The IER is defined as the amount of time it takes for information to travel from one point to another around the globe. The KPR refers to the amount of information created every minute of the day. To understand the power of storytelling, it is worthwhile to momentarily reflect on the changing landscapes over the centuries and the subsequent impact on the narrative. For example, in 1450 the invention of the printing press led to the invention of periodicals and the novel. Over 400 years later, the creation of the motion picture camera served as the inspiration for the development of feature films. By the second decade of the twentieth century, radio and television created audio and visual possibilities for people to share stories. By the 1990s, the Internet had introduced an entirely new way of communicating electronically and would forever change how people created, told, and shared stories. The Internet is the first communication medium with the capability of acting like the previous forms of media since it allows one to create text, audio, or video. Moreover, today's stories are created, told, and shared online with billions of people around the world simultaneously. The agile manager needs to understand how the invention of each new medium allowed the IER to decrease while increasing the KPR; that is, the time it took for information to travel around the world decreased (IER) while the amount of knowledge being produced on a daily basis increased (KPR). Fast forward to today, the IER is now real-time and the KPR is so high is practically incomprehensible to understand just how much information is produced daily. As Thomas Friedman of *The New York Times* noted, "Thanks to cloud computing, robotics, 3G wireless connectivity, Skype, Facebook, Google, LinkedIn, Twitter, the iPad, and cheap Internet-enabled smartphones, the world has gone from connected to hyper-connected."[15]

According to the consulting firm Collage Group, "the proliferation of screens, rise of social media, and creation of new digital media outlets have all converged to create unprecedented (consumer) stimulation."[16] As N. J. Falk wrote in *Forbes*, new "established brands are now faced with an unparalleled challenge as they struggle to break through the social and media noise to engage their audience in today's fractured ecosystem operating in an ever more complex landscape."[17] To illustrate today's fractured ecosystem following are a few statistical highlights from the infographic "What Happens In An Internet Minute in 2020":

- 1.9 million texts sent
- 4.7 million YouTube videos viewed
- 4.1 million search queries
- $1.1 million spent online
- 694,000 people scrolling Instagram
- 190 million emails sent[18]

[15] Friedman, T.L. 2011. "A Theory of Everything (Sort Of)." *The New York Times,* August 13, 2011. https://nytimes.com/2011/08/14/opinion/sunday/Friedman-a-theory-of-everyting-sort-of.html

[16] "Breaking through the Clutter: Advertising that Works with Gen-Z & Millennials (Part 1)." *Collage Group*, https://collagegroup.com/2018/02/22/ads-millennials-gen-z/

[17] Falk, N.J. 2019. "Through the Noise: How to Build Brand Engagement In A Cluttered Digital Landscape." *Forbes,* February 28, 2019. https://forbes.com/sites/njgoldston/2019/02/28/10-ways-to-break-through-the-noise-how-to-build-brand-engagement-in-a-cluttered-digital-landscape/#423c5e0467b1

[18] Lewis, L. 2020. "Infographic: What Happens In An Internet Minute 2020." March 10, 2020. https://allaccess.com/merge/archive/31294/infographic-what-happens-in-an-internet-minute

These statistics, and many more, illustrate this collision of the IER and KPR. With more information being produced and distributed faster than ever before, the agile manager operating in a volatile world needs to understand the necessity of advocating for their organization by creating clear, concise, and compelling stories to share with different audiences. There is already ample evidence on the effectiveness of storytelling via social media platforms. For example, according to a 2020 report by Spout Social, "stories have been one of the biggest social media trends of the past couple of years and 2020 looks to be no different as interactive stories and polls are brilliant ways to go back and forth with your audience."[19] Unfortunately, far too many leaders still fail to practice this second principle of advocacy.

Carol Kinsey Goman noted, "leaders are missing the opportunity to employ a crucial communication strategy if they aren't telling stories. Stories are a potent force for building community, capturing the imagination, and exerting influence."[20] Writing in *Forbes*, Celinne Da Costa noted, "while every business has a story to tell, too many fail at doing so with marketing communication that is clear, captivating and effective."[21] The numerous social media platforms available today offer managers a free and easy-to-use way to stick in the minds of consumers in an ever-growing crowded marketplace. Nick Morgan, author of *Power Cues: The Subtle Science of Leading Groups, Persuading Others, and Maximizing Your Personal Impact*, believes in the power of stories and wrote: "Facts and figures and all the rational things that we think are important in the business world actually don't stick in our minds at all…but telling stories allows the leader to create 'sticky' memories by attaching emotions" to

[19] Barnhart, B. 2020. "The Most Important Social Media Trends to Know for 2020." *Spout Social*, May 6, 2020. https://sproutsocial.com/insights/social-media-trends/

[20] Goman, C.K. 2012. "Why Leaders Should Tell Stories." *Forbes*, May 14, 2012. https://forbes.com/sites/carolkinseygoman/2012/05/14/why-leaders-should-tell-stories/#24340d913b3f

[21] Costa, C.D. 2017. "Why Every Business Needs Powerful Storytelling To Grow." *Forbes*, December 19, 2017. https://forbes.com/sites/celinnedacosta/2017/12/19/why-every-business-needs-powerful-storytelling-to-grow/#2a74c5cf43b0

people, events, and places.[22] Agile managers who can learn how to create, share, and maintain good storytelling over time will have a significant advantage over others.

The agile manager as an advocate who tells stories should recall the observation of Randy Shattuck who wrote, "when leaders tell the right stories at the right time and in the right way, they help create clarity and resolve in the people who follow them."[23] Such clarity and resolve can help fuel the engine of change an organization needs to use as it seeks to achieve and sustain growth in a volatile world. Telling stories (Principle #14) allows the manager a powerful tool as they deepen their understanding of today's realities and tomorrow's possibilities, appreciate the technology and market forces disrupting change, and commit to focused and incremental progress.[24] "With 90 percent of the world's data having been produced in the last two years and more than 26 billion smart devices in circulation,"[25] the agile manager as advocate needs to tell clear, concise, and compelling stories to help their organization "stand out in an increasingly competitive digital marketplace."[26] If, as previously discussed, the first duty of a leader is to define reality, the agile manager should do so by telling stories about today's realities and tomorrow's possibilities on a variety of social media platforms (Principle #15).

---

[22] O'Hara, C. 2014. "How to Tell a Great Story." *Harvard Business Review,* July 30, 2014. https://hbr.org/2014/07/how-to-tell-a-great-story

[23] Shattuck, R. 2017. "Why It's Important for Great Leaders to Tell Great Stories." *Forbes,* September 26, 2017. https://forbes.com/sites/forbesagency-council/2017/09/26/why-its-important-for-great-leaders-to-tell-great-stories/#7e917c596f99

[24] "Tech Trends 2020." *Deloitte Insights,* https://www2.deloitte.com/content/dam/Deloitte/pt/Documents/tech-trends/TechTrends2020.pdf

[25] "2020 Global Marketing Trends: Bringing Authenticity to our Digital Age." Deloitte Insights. https://www2.deloitte.com/content/dam/Deloitte/uk/Documents/consultancy/deloitte-uk-consulting-global-marketing-trends.pdf

[26] Jones, L. 2020. "Work in the 2020s: 5 Essential Skills to Succeed." *Financial Times,* January 5, 2020. https://ft.com/content/74d3c16a-1f35-11ea-92da-f0c92e957a96

Principle #15: Diversify Channels

In addition to creating content (Principle #13) and telling stories (Principle #14), the agile manager as an advocate can also diversify the channels (Principle #15) of their material and narratives. Moving beyond well-established silos and recognizing their organization operates within a broad digital ecosystem remains a critical function of any manager looking to increase an organization's agility. The ongoing, disruptive, and innovative digital landscape continues to offer organizations new avenues to connect with employees, customers, and partners. Leveraging as many communication channels within the digital ecosystem can help the agile manager build, enhance, and deepen relationships with internal and external stakeholders. "CEOs should be company advocates themselves and can do so by using social media to their advantage, and CEOs should create an employee advocacy program that trains their employees on how to use their own social media networks to both grow the business and amplify its reach."[27] The diversity of digital networks, the ever-growing digital ecosystem, and the impact of social platforms are all the result of explosive growth associated with the number of people online around the world during the last three decades.

Understanding the rate and depth of the number of people around the world online illustrates just how VUCA today's global marketplace has become. Prior to 1990 concepts such as the Internet, global connectivity, and digital ecosystem were in the nascent stages of development. For example, in 1990 a mere 2.6 million people accessed the Internet. During the last 30 years, the number of people online around the world experienced exponential growth:

- 1990: 2.6 million
- 1995: 44 million
- 2000: 412 million
- 2005: 1 billion

---

[27] Fisher, J. 2020. "Social Leadership: What CEOs Need to Know." *Forbes*, April 3, 2020. https://forbes.com/sites/forbescoachescouncil/2020/04/03/social-leadership-what-ceos-need-to-know/#4c612f3d49b7

- 2010: 1.9 billion
- 2015: 3.4 billion[28]
- 2020: 4.6 billion

In 30 short years, the world witnessed the number of people online grow from less than three million to four and a half billion! Will the trend continue? Most likely. During the 2019 to 2020 period, the number of people around the world using the Internet has grown to 4.62 billion, an increase of 7 percent (298 million new users) compared to January 2019.[29] With the United Nations projecting global population to reach 9.7 billion by 2050,[30] the number of people online around the world is projected to reach 7.5 billion by 2030 (90 percent of the projected world population of 8.5 billion, 6 years of age and older).[31] With more people around the world online, the number of users across the social media ecosystem is also expected to increase.

Worldwide, there are 3.80 billion social media users in January 2020, with this number increasing by more than 9 percent (321 million new users) since January 2019. [32] As of April 2020 the top 15 social media platforms that each have 300 million or more monthly active users are as follows:[33]

1. Facebook has 2.498 billion monthly active users.
2. YouTube has 2 billion monthly active users.
3. WhatsApp has 2 billion monthly active users.

---

[28] Our World In Data, no date. https://ourworldindata.org/internet

[29] Internet World Stats, https://internetworldstats.com/stats.htm. Date accessed June 11, 2020.

[30] United Nations, press release dated June 17, 2019. https://un.org/development/desa/en/news/population/world-population-prospects-2019.html

[31] Morgan, S. 2019. "Humans On The Internet Will Triple From 2015 To 2022 And Hit 6 Billion." *Cybercrime Magazine*, July 18, 2019. https://cybersecurityventures.com/how-many-internet-users-will-the-world-have-in-2022-and-in-2030/

[32] "Digital 2020: Global Digital Overview." January 30, 2020. https://wearesocial.com/blog/2020/01/digital-2020-3-8-billion-people-use-social-media

[33] Global Social Media Overview. https://datareportal.com/social-media-users (accessed on June 11, 2020).

4. Facebook Messenger has 1.3 billion monthly active users.

5. WeChat (Weixin) has 1.165 billion monthly active users.

6. Instagram has 1 billion monthly active users.

7. TikTok (Douyin) has 800 million monthly active users.

8. QQ has 731 million monthly active users.

9. QZone has 517 million monthly active users.

10. Sina Weibo has 516 million monthly active users.

11. Reddit has 430 million monthly active users.

12. Kuaishou has 400 million monthly active users

13. Snapchat's potential advertising reach is roughly 398 million active users.

14. Twitter's potential advertising reach is roughly 386 million active users.

15. Pinterest has 366 million monthly active users.

With billions now on social media platforms, daily time consumption continues to change. For example, social media users are now spending an average of 2 hours and 24 minutes per day multinetworking across an average of eight social networks and messaging apps.[34] Facebook is most popular, where people spend an average of 2 hours and 24 minutes each day, YouTube takes an average of 40 minutes per day and Pinterest users take it slow and scroll through ideas for only 14.2 minutes every day.[35] Any organization looking to achieve and sustain growth for any period of time needs managers who understand how the world is changing and the implications of those developments. Failure to recognize the dynamics of a world in constant motion could result in an organization that learns firsthand just how quickly it can become irrelevant. One dynamic requiring additional research is the escalating relevance of the 5.19 billion people using mobile phones around the globe.[36] As detailed in The State of Mobile 2020 report "Consumers averaged 3 hours and 40 minutes on

---

[34] Chaffey, D. 2020. "Global Social Media Research Summary 2020." *Smart Insights*, April 17, 2020. https://smartinsights.com/social-media-marketing/social-media-strategy/new-global-social-media-research/

[35] "How Much Time Do People Spend on Social Media in 2020?" June 11, 2020. https://techjury.net/blog/time-spent-on-social-media/#gre

[36] "Digital 2020: Global Digital Overview." January 30, 2020. https://wearesocial.com/blog/2020/01/digital-2020-3-8-billion-people-use-social-media

mobile in 2019, up 35% since 2017; and companies from every verti-
cal are benefiting by making mobile the center of their digital transformation investments."[37] The key word there is "transformation" as many
organizations still lack the agility required to adapt and remain relevant.
Understand how customers use the various social media platforms is
foundational to understanding the importance of advocating on an array
of options in the digital ecosystem.

Social media's ubiquitous presence in the daily lives of billions has
completely changed how customers, employees, and other stakeholders
interact with organizations. Since more people are accessing social media
platforms via mobile devices, managers looking to drive agility in their
organization need to understand the new interactivity patterns of customers.[38] The current generation of mobile devices make it effortless for
customers to find brands they use, discover new ones, or interact with
other customers when a buying decision is at hand. Social media also
offers valuable community-building opportunities like "the Chick-fil-A
Instagram channel that brings to life the Chick-fil-A brand and puts an
experience right at our fans' fingertips."[39]

The manager in a volatile world looking to enhance their organization's agility needs to find a way to leverage the connectivity, power, and
relevance of social media to stay focused on creating interactive opportunities for customers.[40] Central for any interactive opportunity on any
social media platform is the concept of "social listening." Research has
confirmed nearly two-thirds of marketers identified social listening as the

---

[37] "The State of Mobile 2020." *App Annie,* https://appannie.com/en/go/state-
of-mobile-2020/?utm_source=digital-2020&utm_medium=partnership&utm_
campaign=ww-logo-201910-1910-digital-2020-partnership&utm_
content=report-&sfdcid=7016F000002MS1c

[38] Droesch, B. 2019. "More Than Half of US Social Network Users Will Be
Mobile-Only in 2019." eMarketer, April 26, 2019. https://emarketer.com/
content/more-than-half-of-social-network-users-will-be-mobile-only-in-2019

[39] Chick-fil-A Instagram Experience, no date, https://shortyawards.com/8th/
chick-fil-as-instagram-experience

[40] Gotter, A. 2020. "The 6 Marketing Channels You Should Prioritize in 2020."
Disruptive Advertising, February 11, 2020. https://disruptiveadvertising.com/
marketing/marketing-channels/

most significant issue for managers serving as advocates in the future. The most agile of marketing managers, for example, are prioritizing what's being said rather than how many people are talking or looking at a single post. Long-term engagement, rather than a short-term spike in "likes," is slowly becoming the single greatest attribute for organizations looking to achieve sustainability. "Rather than chase a viral moment, brands are rightfully trying to understand what's driving conversations with custom-ers."[41] This shift, from the momentarily number of likes to long-term engagement, demonstrates real-time agility as managers strive to remain relevant through advocacy.

The consulting firm Deloitte identified seven trends related to social media engagement in 2020: purpose, human experience, fusion, trust, participation, talent, and agility. To remain relevant and sustain growth, organizations need managers who understand how to leverage these seven trends to create an engaged digital ecosystem for all stakeholders. Failing to do so in an authentic manner will jeopardize trust across the vari-ous platforms operating in the ecosystem.[42] As Peter Aceto CEO, ING DIRECT observed, "Successful leaders will no longer be measured just by stock price. Managing and communicating with shareholders, employ-ees, government, community, customers will be table stakes in the future. They are talking about your business anyway. Why not be included in the conversation?"[43] Herein lies the critical foundation for the agile manager in a volatile world serving as an advocate for their organization. What are you doing to be included in the conversation about your organiza-tion on the different social media platforms? The agile manager needs to understand "a company's executives are among the most valuable tools in its marketing arsenal when it comes to moving the dial on company

[41] Barnhart, B. 2020. "The Most Important Social Media Trends to Know for 2020." *Spout Social.* https://sproutsocial.com/insights/social-media-trends/

[42] "2020 Global Marketing Trends: Bringing Authenticity to our Digital Age." *Deloitte Insights,* https://www2.deloitte.com/content/dam/Deloitte/uk/Docu-ments/consultancy/deloitte-uk-consulting-global-marketing-trends.pdf

[43] The Social CEO: Executives Tell All, 2012 report, https://webershandwick. com/uploads/news/files/Social-CEO-Study.pdf

objectives."[44] Such engagement across platforms can ultimately help the agile manager function as a pioneer exploring new ideas for products and services that inspire employees and customers alike.

Questions

Principle #13: Create Content

- How often do you advocate for your organization, employees, or customers via creating content?
- How can creating content demonstrate agility?
- What skills, traits, or habits could you leverage to create content?
- If you do not create content, why is that?
- If you have created content what has been your experience?
- Do you believe creating content is irrelevant or an unnecessary distraction?
- Have you spent any time reading the content of other leaders who publish their material online or on social media?

Principle #14: Tell Stories

- What stories have had the great impact in your life? Why?
- What is the last story you told about your organization?
- How often do you tell stories about your organization?
- What are three stories you might tell about your organization?
- What channels of communication do you currently use to hear or read about stories?
- Does your organization support storytelling?
- Would telling stories impact the culture?
- What do you think is the relationship between storytelling and agility?
- Do your competitors use stories? If so, how, and what have you learned from studying them?

---

[44] Clinton, E. 2019. "How Many Fortune 500 CEOs are on Social Media?." March 3, 2019. https://influentialexecutive.com/fortune-500-ceos-on-social/

Principle #15: Diversify Channels

- What social media outlets do you use to advocate for your organization?
- Do you allow employees to post on social media during the day?
- Is what is being shared on the different channels representative of the organizational culture?
- What channels are most used by your employees?
- What are your competitors doing on the different social media channels?
- Does your organization offer any training on helping managers learn about social media?
- How can you improve your role as an advocate on different platforms?

CHAPTER 8

Pioneer

Introduction to Function #6: Pioneer

The etymology of the word *pioneer* stems from the early sixteenth century referring to a military term denoting a member of the infantry originating from the French *pionnier* or "foot soldier." For those looking to create a more agile organization to sustain itself in a volatile world, they should consider pioneer as the sixth function of an agile manager. The agile manager as a pioneer identifies issues, explores new solutions, and inspires others with a vision where the organization remains vibrant, relevant, and essential. To that end, the agile manager as a pioneer has three principles to consider. An agile manager should encourage dialogue from employees and others about the organization's products and services (Principle #16). During the dialogue, an agile manager should remain open-minded about new ideas (Principle #17). This encouragement of open dialogue and consideration of new ideas can help the agile manager inspire others as the organization looks to move forward in today's volatile world (Principle #18).

Failure to function as a pioneer jeopardizes an organization's relevance. As David Robinson wrote in his BBC article, "to avoid fossilization, you need to embrace evolution; and to do that one needs to ensure every manager is open to the potential of new innovations."[1] History offers so many examples of managers who failed to function as pioneers that researchers have coined such a phenomenon the "competency trap." This competency trap occurs when a company lacks the agility to balance the exploitation of their existing products with the

---

[1] Robinson, D. 2020. "How to Avoid the 'Competency Trap.'" *BBC*, June 8, 2020. https://www.bbc.com/worklife/article/20200608-what-is-the-competency-trap

exploration of future opportunities. Kodak is one such example of a company whose expertise was so entrenched that it ruined any capacity to deal with a changing and uncertain market. For over 100 years, Kodak dominated the analog photography market. Despite being the first company to create a digital camera, however, "so many of its workers were entrenched in the analogue industry and struggled to see and exploit the potential of digital processing."[2] Eventually Kodak filed for bankruptcy in 2011 and emerged two years later as a shell of its former self. Xerox is another big business whose managers failed to function as pioneers. Xerox invented the first personal computer and their product was way ahead of its time. "Unfortunately, the management thought going digital would be too expensive and they never bothered to exploit the opportunities before them."[3]

Despite the myriad of historical examples, scholarly publications, and case studies, most managers and leaders lack the ability, or fortitude, to function as a pioneer. Challenging the status quo, communicating vision in a compelling manner, and translating one's thoughts into reality are simply too overwhelming for managers at all levels. In the best-selling book *The Leadership Challenge: How to Make Extraordinary Things Happen in Organizations*, two leading scholars James M. Kouzes and Barry Z. Posner noted the leader as pioneer function when they wrote, "Leaders are pioneers—people who are willing to step out into the unknown. They search for opportunities to innovate, grow, and improve."[4] Pioneers are agents of change. To sustain growth in a volatile world, the agile manager needs to understand their function as a pioneer is to challenge the status quo. Kouzes and Posner noted, "Every single personal-best leadership case we collected involved some change from the status quo. Not one person

---

[2] Robinson, D. 2020. "How to Avoid the 'Competency Trap.'" *BBC*, June 8, 2020. https://www.bbc.com/worklife/article/20200608-what-is-the-competency-trap

[3] Lagerstedt, E. 2018. "50 examples of Companies that Failed to Innovate." December 9, 2018. https://inquentia.com/50-examples-of-companies-that-failed-to-innovate/

[4] Kouzes, J.M., and B.Z. Posner. 2003. *The Jossey-Bass Academic Administrator's Guide to Exemplary Leadership*. Jossey-Bass. https://www.amazon.com/Jossey-Bass-Academic-Administrators-Exemplary-Leadership/dp/0787966649

claimed to have achieved a personal best by keeping things the same. All leaders challenge the process."[5]

In their research, Suzanne M. Johnson Vickberg and Kim Christfort identified four types of leaders: pioneers (36 percent of leaders exhibited this type), drivers (29 percent), integrators (18 percent), and guardians (17 percent).[6] "Pioneers value possibilities, and spark energy," the researchers noted. Additionally, pioneers believe risks are worth taking, drive imagination on their teams, focus on the big picture, and are drawn to bold new ideas and creative approaches. Since they prioritize action over thought sometime, pioneers tend to be spontaneous and outgoing. They think quickly and speak energetically, sometimes before thinking much at all.[7] Robbie Bach echoed similar sentiment about leaders as pioneers when he wrote, "being a pioneer requires an intense focus on growth and taking territory from the competition—as such it requires a certain relentless pursuit of success at the expense of others. It is not for the faint of heart or for the gentle of soul."[8] Such an intense focus on growth requires the encouragement of dialogue (Principle #16) to openly and freely discuss critical issues, questions, and concerns related to the organization's ability to become more agile and sustain growth.

Principle #16: Encourage Dialogue

Encouraging dialogue is the first of three principles related to the agile manager as a pioneer. Pioneers are visionaries. Pioneers venture into the unknown. Pioneers have the high level of self-awareness required to

---

[5] Kouzes, J.M., and B.Z. Posner. 2003. *The Jossey-Bass Academic Administrator's Guide to Exemplary Leadership*. Jossey-Bass. https://www.amazon.com/Jossey-Bass-Academic-Administrators-Exemplary-Leadership/dp/0787966649

[6] Johnson Vickberg, S.M. and K. Christfort. 2017. "Pioneers, Drivers, Integrators, and Guardians." *Harvard Business Review,* March 2017. https://hbr.org/2017/03/the-new-science-of-team-chemistry

[7] Johnson Vickberg, S.M. and K. Christfort. 2017. "Pioneers, Drivers, Integrators, and Guardians." *Harvard Business Review,* March 2017. https://hbr.org/2017/03/the-new-science-of-team-chemistry

[8] Bach, R. 2019. "Are You an Explorer, A Pioneer, or a Settler?" *LinkedIn*, June 17, 2019. https://www.linkedin.com/pulse/you-explorer-pioneer-settler-robbie-bach/

see what others are unable to and to navigate unchartered waters. Leadership qualities in a volatile world, however, must extend well beyond being a visionary. The ability to achieve and maintain dialogue is at the heart of being a successful leader today. In a 2020 report LinkedIn noted creativity, collaboration, persuasion, and emotional intelligence as the top four soft skills organizations need to succeed today.[9] Each of these four soft skills demonstrate how people work with one another, bring new ideas to the table, and communicate in different modalities. Moreover, the organizations that benefit from these soft skills have managers who encourage dialogue where people feel comfortable exhibiting their creativity, collaboration, persuasion, and emotional intelligence. To highlight the significance of dialogue to the manager functioning as a pioneer, Rodger Dean Duncan noted in *Forbes*: "You may have excellent technical skills. You may even be innovative and visionary. But if you do not know how to *engage* people, you're toast. The best leaders (regardless of title or lack thereof) have good people skills."[10] While people skills is often synonymous with emotional intelligence, it also involves understanding, practicing, and inviting people to engage in one of the four ways of talking as defined by researchers Robert Garmston and Bruce Wellman:

- *Conversation*—a casual chat about personal and social matters.
- *Discussion*—a purposeful talk with a purpose; often to decide.
- *Debate*—an extreme form of discussion where people advocate for specific sides.
- *Dialogue*—more structured than conversation, but less structured than discussion or debate.[11]

---

[9] Deanna (Lazzaroni) Pate. 2020. "The Skills Companies Need Most in 2020—and How to Learn Them." *LinkedIn*, January 13, 2020. https://learning.linkedin.com/blog/top-skills/the-skills-companies-need-most-in-2020and-how-to-learn-them

[10] Duncan, R.D. 2018. "Leadership as Dialogue, Not Monologue." *Forbes*, August 7, 2018. https://www.forbes.com/sites/rodgerdeanduncan/2018/08/07/leadership-as-dialogue-not-monologue/#3cbd46e7c797

[11] Graybill, O., and L.B. Easton. 2015. "The Art of Dialogue." *Educational Leadership*, April 2015. www.ascd.org/publications/educational-leadership/apr15/vol72/num07/The-Art-of-Dialogue.aspx

Dialogue operates differently from the other avenues of talking because it provides learning opportunities, allows others to have a voice, and offers different perspectives. Managing people today requires a recognition, application, and assessment of the four ways of talking. Some situations require a conversation while others a dialogue or debate. Additionally, "when a group is trying to make a decision, it may still want to engage in dialogue to explore ideas, and then shift to discussion."[12] Knowing when to use which way of talking can make all the difference for the manager looking to enhance an organization's agility. This is especially true for an organization that achieved some level of success. "The greater your success, the more you need to stay in touch with fresh opinions and perspectives and welcome honest feedback."[13] The need for dialogue will be an important one for managers to understand, address, and assess if they hope to increase an organization's agility.[14]

One solution to encourage dialogue would be to invite employees to work within a different department for a few months. Opening their eyes to the various functional areas of the organization can prove to be a much-needed catalyst to loosen the cognitive rigidity associated with doing the same job in one department for any length of time. Such an exercise can also introduce the agile mindset required to have the organization make the necessary adjustments in sustain itself. Since 45 percent of human capital and C-suite leaders said that digital transformation was moving too fast and that they were unable to keep up, helping employees understand the different functional areas and how they interact with one another can support an organization's efforts to become more agile.[15] Additionally,

---

[12] Graybill, O., and L.B. Easton. 2015. "The Art of Dialogue." *Educational Leadership,* April 2015. www.ascd.org/publications/educational-leadership/apr15/vol72/num07/The-Art-of-Dialogue.aspx

[13] Hyacinth, B. 2018. "Never Punish Loyal Employees for Being Honest." *Linked,* July 18, 2018. https://www.linkedin.com/pulse/never-punish-loyal-employees-being-honest-brigette-hyacinth/

[14] Groysberg, B., and M. Slind. 2012. "Leadership is a Conversation." *Harvard Business Review,* June 2012. https://hbr.org/2012/06/leadership-is-a-conversation

[15] "Business Agility Critical to Post-Pandemic Workforce, Economic Recovery." June 24, 2020. https://huntscanlon.com/business-agility-critical-to-post-pandemic-workforce-economic-recovery/

dialogue can afford managers opportunities to listen to junior employees who often have a naïve, but oftentimes fresh, perspective on the organization. Such a dialogue would serve as a demonstration of management encouraging employees to question the underlying assumptions behind an organization's decision making. "What is crucial is to have ways to challenge the status quo, to inject variation in the corporate DNA," says Loizos Heracleous at Warwick Business School in the UK.[16] In today's VUCA global marketplace, "traditional corporate communication must give way to a process that is more dynamic and more sophisticated" involving an open, clear, and transparent dialogue.[17]

For an organization to enhance its agility, managers need to encourage dialogue and deepen their understanding of issues, questions, and concerns. The function of pioneer provides opportunities for the manager to engage in a dialogue that invites discovery. Unlike the adversarial form of debate, a dialogue illuminates the common values shared among managers and employees alike and allows individuals to express their own interests, ask questions, and reevaluate their assumptions. "Honest and open communication is an essential ingredient in maintaining a successful company," noted Peter Economy in *Inc.*[18] This essential ingredient can allow an organization to respond to fast-changing market conditions and agile competitors. Economy suggests to "give employees an incentive to speak up such as a simple thank you, some type of reward, or even more authority and responsibility if possible."[19] Encouraging dialogue allows the manager as pioneer to foster a growth in understanding,

---

[16] Robinson, D. 2020. "How to Avoid the 'Competency Trap.'" *BBC*, June 8, 2020. https://www.bbc.com/worklife/article/20200608-what-is-the-competency-trap

[17] Groysberg, B., and M. Slind. 2012. "Leadership is a Conversation." *Harvard Business Review,* June 2012. https://hbr.org/2012/06/leadership-is-a-conversation%20%20

[18] Peter Economy. 2013. "5 Ways to Get Your Employees to Speak Up." *Inc.*, October 3, 2013. https://www.inc.com/peter-economy/5-ways-to-get-your-employees-to-speak-up.html

[19] Peter Economy. 2013. "5 Ways to Get Your Employees to Speak Up." *Inc.*, October 3, 2013. https://www.inc.com/peter-economy/5-ways-to-get-your-employees-to-speak-up.html

a commitment to remain open-minded, and a decision to act together so the organization can achieve the level of agility required to sustain growth in a volatile world.

Encouraging dialogue allows "an agile leader to listen to their team, their markets, partners, clients and even competitors. They are ready to hear what needs to be heard and then do something meaningful with that information."[20] To encourage dialogue agile managers in a volatile world can refer to the following set of characteristics identified by researchers Jennifer Ness and Peter W. Williams[21]

- Consideration of different perspectives while engaging in the dialogue
- Identification of the purpose, nature, and intent of the dialogue
- Distribution of ground rules for sharing, listening, and discussing information
- Creation of a safe zone to speak openly without fear of ridicule
- Formation of a sense of belonging and inclusion for all involved

These ground rules provide a blueprint for managers to follow who are trying to adjust their communication styles in a world characterized by innovative digital technologies that continue to disrupt global commerce. To create the level of change required in a volatile world, leaders need to maintain an ongoing dialogue with internal and external stakeholders to drive continuous positive change and affect the required change. This new level of engagement via dialogue is predicated upon the manager creating a space where power, position, and politics are diminished or suspended, As Ness and Williams concluded, "in such spaces, conversations are between equals, and the thoughts and assumptions held by all stakeholders can be

---

[20] "15 Key Qualities that define an agile leader," *Forbes*, June 17, 2020. https://www.forbes.com/sites/forbescoachescouncil/2020/06/17/15-key-qualities-that-define-an-agile-leader/#55ae18ce7f31

[21] Ness, J., and P.W. Williams. 2009. "Dialogue Management Factors: A 2010 Vancouver Winter Olympic and Paralympic Games case." *Journal of Teaching in Travel & Tourism* 8, nos. 2–3, 193–221. http://dx.doi.org/10.1080/15313220802634166

confronted, discussed, and explored in a constructive fashion."[22] Such a process, however, requires the agile manager as pioneer to know when to talk, when to listen, and to always remain open-minded (Principle #17).

Principle #17: Remain Open-Minded

The facilitation and encouragement of dialogue (Principle #16) requires a manager who recognizes, understands, and demonstrates the ability to remain open-minded (Principle #17). Failing to consider new ideas in a volatile world is a shortcut to jeopardizing one's sustainability. As Wendy Handson from BetterManager noted, "We need to be agile now more than ever. As our work and environment change on a regular basis, being agile is being open to shifting, getting feedback and beginning again."[23] Writing in *Harvard Business Review*, Al Pittampalli identified three leaders who operate in a volatile world by considering "emerging evidence and changing their minds accordingly provides extraordinary advantages." Alan Mulally of Ford Motor Company remains skeptical of his own opinions, hedge fund billionaire Ray Dalio insists his team second-guess his thinking and Christine Lagarde of the European Central Bank seeks out information to disprove her beliefs.[24] For the pioneering manager looking to increase their organization's agility in a volatile world, remaining open-minded, while difficult to achieve at times, offers managers a viable option.

Two strategies people use to remain open-minded and acquire new view, information, or knowledge are assimilation and accommodation.

---

[22] Ness, J., and P.W. Williams. 2009. "Dialogue Management Factors: A 2010 Vancouver Winter Olympic and Paralympic Games case," *Journal of Teaching in Travel & Tourism* 8, nos. 2–3, 193–221. http://dx.doi.org/10.1080/15313220802634166

[23] "15 Key qualities that Define an Agile Leader." *Forbes*, June 17, 2020. https://www.forbes.com/sites/forbescoachescouncil/2020/06/17/15-key-qualities-that-define-an-agile-leader/#55ae18ce7f31

[24] Pittampalli, A. 2016. "The Best Leaders Allow Themselves to be Persuaded." *Harvard Business Review*, March 3, 2016. https://hbr.org/2016/03/the-best-leaders-allow-themselves-to-be-persuaded?cm_mmc=email-_-newsletter-_-management_tip-_-tip_date&referral=00203&utm_source=newsletter_management_tip&utm_medium=email&utm_campaign=tip_date

Assimilation of knowledge occurs when a learner encounters a new idea and they "fit" that idea into what they already know. Accommodation of knowledge, however, is more substantial, requiring the learner to reshape their previously held beliefs. An oft-used analogy to describe the two approaches involves a balloon. Assimilation is like adding air into a balloon; the more air you add in the bigger it gets. The balloon, or in this case the mind, expands in proportion to the amount of air, information, one adds to it. Accommodation, however, requires one to do something with the information acquired through assimilation. Accommodation challenges one to remain open-minded and turn the round balloon into the shape of an animal. Herein lies the problem with professionals who have worked in one industry, or perhaps in one organization, for decades. They have assimilated so much information they become incapable of accommodating new ways of thinking. In other words, closed-minded individuals lack the agility, vision, and imagination to transform a balloon into a different shape. This lack of agile mindedness offers an important lesson for managers operating in a volatile world as they may have access to information or knowledge but lack any capacity to create actionable intelligence. Remaining open-minded through either assimilation or accommodation requires one to suspend judgment temporarily, to weigh information free of bias, and to recognize their existing beliefs as incorrect or in need of new frames of reference.

Such a process, however, often involves cognitive dissonance, the mental stress experienced while simultaneously holding two or more contradictory beliefs, ideas, or values at the same time. Cognitive dissonance frequently requires one to travel outside of their comfort zone and push the boundaries of intelligence to consider completely opposite ideas. Managers operating in a volatile world looking to increase their organization's agility need to be comfortable with cognitive dissonance as disruptive forces will continue to challenge long-held beliefs, assumptions, and thoughts. As F. Scott Fitzgerald wrote in 1936, "the test of a first-rate intelligence is the ability to hold two opposed ideas in the mind at the same time, and still retain the ability to function."[25] Using Benjamin Franklin as a case study,

---

[25] Fitzgerald, F.S. 1936. "The Crack Up." *Esquire*, February 1936. https://esquire.com/lifestyle/a4310/the-crack-up/#ixzz1Fvs5lu8w

author Shane Snow discussed how Franklin knew he was smarter than most of his contemporaries but also recognized there was much he could still learn. Franklin's opening statement would often include the phrase, "I could be wrong, but..." This strategy, according to Snow, "put people at ease, helped them to take disagreements less personally and helped Franklin to psychologically prime himself to be open to new ideas."[26]

As Julia Carter wrote, "Today's disruption requires open-minded leaders who can help businesses build new business models and help organizations navigate a path for all to follow."[27] Doing so will help the manager who wishes to function as a pioneer and help their organization evolve as the speed of disruption continues to alter the very fabric of almost every industry. For the manager hesitant to remain open-minded, it would behoove them to remember this simple adage "a close mind will most likely result in a closed business." Relying on the old tried and tested methods for success are either going to be redundant or have adverse effects on the bottom line. Remaining open-minded and receptive to new ideas, however, allows the agile manager to ensure their organization stays ahead of the curve. Managers who remain open-minded are less likely to get stuck in a rut, more likely to become naturally inquisitive, and better able to reinterpret traditional products and services. For the manager looking to increase their organization's agility, asking questions remains an effective tool to remain inquisitive and open-minded.

Open-minded managers are comfortable asking questions. They recognize, accept, and understand their limitations in terms of knowledge, perspective, and process. When managers attend meetings, they engage in a dialogue and ask questions that can help them better understand someone else's situation. In a volatile world marked by constant disruption having the self-awareness to remain open-minded is a critical function of the pioneering manager looking to create a more agile organization.

---

[26] Snow, S. 2018. "A New Way to Become More Open-Minded." *Harvard Business Review,* November 20, 2018. https://hbr.org/2018/11/a-new-way-to-become-more-open-minded

[27] Carter, J. 2018. "4 Benefits of Being an Open-Minded Leader." *LinkedIn,* December 21, 2018. https://www.linkedin.com/pulse/4-benefits-being-open-minded-leader-julia-carter-virtual-team-trainer/

Unfortunately, many managers lack self-awareness, leverage their power and authority over others, and exhibit close-minded tendencies. As such, these managers never ask people their opinion, fail to ask questions in general, and approach ever situation with a mindset of figuring out how to exploit someone else. Unlike the open-minded manager who remains curious, the close-minded person lacks any capacity to engage with others. As Julian Baggini wrote, "everyone likes to think they are open-minded. However, even those of us that actively invite different ideas rarely allow them to set up home. There's plenty of research that suggests our fundamental beliefs don't generally change much once we're in our twenties."[28] For the agile manager operating in a volatile world, however, they will need to increase their self-awareness so they can break out of their normal thinking patterns to identify innovative solutions.

One of the hurdles for the agile manager to acknowledge they do not know everything and should be open-minded to accepting diverse viewpoints. Inviting, discussing, and considering diverse viewpoints is a hallmark of demonstrating open-mindedness. As Tori Utley wrote in *Forbes*, "Teams offer a diverse number of experiences, views and talents that managers can lean into in order to dive into the unknown, difficult and confusing."[29] According to research conducted by McKinsey, "companies in the top quartile for gender or racial and ethnic diversity are more likely to have financial returns above their national industry medians. Companies in the bottom quartile in these dimensions are statistically less likely to achieve above-average returns. And diversity is probably a competitive differentiator that shifts market share toward more diverse companies over time."[30] It should come as no surprise then that "62% of employers are focusing on hiring for diversity as a means of improving

[28] Baggini, J. 2018. "The Art of Changing Your Mind." *Medium*, October 15, 2018. https://medium.com/@jbaggini/the-art-of-changing-your-mind-76fb3b b75d1d

[29] Utley, T. 2017. "The Importance of Open Dialogue with Your Team." *Forbes*, April 30, 2017. https://forbes.com/sites/toriutley/2017/04/30/the-importance-of-open-dialogue-with-your-team/#2af837fe550e

[30] Hunt, V., D. Layton, and S. Prince. 2015. "Why Diversity Matters." *McKinsey*, January 1, 2015. https://www.mckinsey.com/business-functions/organization/our-insights/why-diversity-matters

company performance and 78% are looking to diversify to help improve company culture," according to a study conducted by LinkedIn.[31] Such diversity of opinions can help drive an organization's curiosity. As Aric Wood of XPLANE noted, "Agility requires adaptability, and adaptability requires the practice of constantly monitoring changing conditions and formulating possible responses. Curiosity is your superpower to solving problems."[32] In today's hypercompetitive, ever changing, and dynamic global marketplace, maintaining such curiosity can then help the agile manager inspire others (Principle #18).

Principle #18: Inspire Others

The 18th and final principle outlined in this publication, and the third and final one associated with the sixth function of an agile manager as pioneer, is inspiring others (Principle #18). The encouragement of open dialogue (Principle #16) with an open mind (Principle #17) by leaders who inspire can help organizations, in the words of Eric Garton, "find ways to constructively disrupt established behaviors and help employees break out of culture-weakening routines."[33] As a manager trying to increase an organization's agility in a volatile situation, take note what one pundit observed: "satisfied employees hold a meeting to discuss what to do about walls, engaged employees begin looking around for ladders to scale the wall, while inspired employees break right through it."[34] Agile managers need to ask themselves if they want their employees to hold meetings, find ladders, or break through the walls preventing the

---

[31] "Global Recruiting Trends, 2018." *LinkedIn.* https://business.linkedin.com/content/dam/me/business/en-us/talent-solutions/resources/pdfs/linkedin-global-recruiting-trends-2018-en-us.pdf

[32] "15 Key Qualities that Define an Agile Leader." *Forbes,* June 17, 2020. https://www.forbes.com/sites/forbescoachescouncil/2020/06/17/15-key-qualities-that-define-an-agile-leader/#55ae18ce7f31

[33] Garton, E. 2017. "How to be an Inspiring Leader." *Harvard Business Review,* April 25, 2017. https://hbr.org/2017/04/how-to-be-an-inspiring-leader

[34] Garton, E., and M. Mankins, 2015. "Engaging your Employees is Good, But Don't Stop There." *Harvard Business Review,* December 9, 2015. https://hbr.org/2015/12/engaging-your-employees-is-good-but-dont-stop-there

organization from making the required forward progress needed to sustain itself. Remember, inspiration comes in many shapes and sizes and is often dependent upon the industry, organization, and situation. There is no one best practice when it comes to inspiring others. What works for one manager may not necessarily work for another. But do remember the Sicilian proverb, *"Il pesce comincia a puzzare dalla testa"* meaning "the fish stinks from the head." In every organization leadership sets the tone for the current climate and vision for the future.

With this principle, it is important to distinguish between the words inspiration and motivation or inspire and motivate. The two words are often used interchangeably, but there are important nuanced differences for the agile manager to note. The first difference stems from the etymology of each word. "Inspire" translates to "in spirit." Inspiration comes from within while "motivate" is an external force that causes one to act. The second difference is motivation pushes one to accomplish a task to earn a reward. The reward is doing the motivation. Inspiration, however, pulls one toward something that stirs the heart, mind, or spirit. While the result is important it is not the focus for one who is inspired. As CEO Marissa Levin wrote, "When we are filled with inspiration, we often do not need external motivation to move forward. The feeling of purpose and meaning is enough to propel us."[35] Just how important is the manager who inspires? According to an IBM survey of 1,700 CEOs through 64 countries, the three most important leadership traits are: (1) the ability to focus intensely on customer needs, (2) the ability to collaborate with colleagues, and (3) the ability to inspire.[36] Moreover, research by Bain and Company found "inspired employees are more than twice as productive as satisfied employees."[37] The examples included here are from three

---

[35] Levin, M. 2017. "Why Great leaders (like Richard Branson) Inspire Instead of Motivate." *Inc.*, March 30, 2017. https://www.inc.com/marissa-levin/why-great-leaders-like-richard-branson-inspire-instead-of-motivate.html

[36] Levin, M. 2017. "Why Great leaders (like Richard Branson) Inspire Instead of Motivate." *Inc.*, March 30, 2017. https://www.inc.com/marissa-levin/why-great-leaders-like-richard-branson-inspire-instead-of-motivate.html

[37] Horwitch, M., and M.W. Callahan. 2016. "How Leaders Inspire: Cracking the Code." Bain & Company, June 9, 2016. https://www.bain.com/insights/how-leaders-inspire-cracking-the-code

completely different companies: Starbucks for coffee, Alcoa for plastics, and Ford for automobiles.

Starbucks CEO Howard Schultz is one example of the agile manager who functioned as a pioneer when his organization needed him most.[38] After a nearly eight-year hiatus, Schultz returned to Starbucks after he realized the organization strayed too far away from its unique customer-focused coffee experience. He encouraged dialogue by inviting people to email him and he personally called stores to see how things were going. He remained open-minded by referring to outside consultants for the first-time and he hired a chief technology officer. By redesigning stores, launching a customer rewards card, and shaking up senior management, Schultz inspired others by demonstrating the high level of agility required for Starbucks to turnaround and sustain growth. Schultz's pioneering efforts resulted in the company's stock, which had cratered 42 percent in 2007, to rebound and gain 143 percent in 2009.[39] Other examples of managers who inspired others include Alcoa's Paul O'Neill and Ford's Alan Mulally.

When Paul O'Neill became CEO of Alcoa in 1987, he understood the value of focusing solely on workplace safety. Much to the chagrin of stockholders upon listening to his first presentation as CEO, O'Neill never wavered, initiated dialogue with employees, and maintained a steadfast commitment to safety. Safety improved dramatically, to the point where Alcoa's worker injury rate fell to 5 percent of the U.S. average. Alcoa's profits would hit a record high during his tenure. "By the time O'Neill retired in 2000 to become Treasury Secretary, the company's annual net income was five times larger than before he arrived, and its market capitalization had risen by $27 billion."[40] When Bill Ford asked long-time Bowing executive Alan Mulally to come to Ford in 2006 to help turn around the business, Mulally knew the company had a macho culture,

---

[38] Groth, A. 2011. "19 Amazing ways CEO Howard Schultz saved Starbucks." *Business Insider*, June 19, 2011. https://www.businessinsider.com/howard-schultz-turned-starbucks-around-2011-6

[39] Meyersohn, N. 2018. "3 Times Howard Schultz saved Starbucks." *CNN Business*, June 5, 2018. https://money.cnn.com/2018/06/05/news/companies/starbucks-howard-schultz-coffee/index.html

[40] "The Power of Safety Leadership: Paul O'Neill, Safety and Alcoa." *AEROssurance*, December 29, 2014. aerossurance.com/helicopters/paul-oneill-safety-alcoa-power-safety-leadership/

forgot its customers, and was running out of money so he took bold action and relied upon 10 Core Values that served him well at Bowing:

1. People first
2. Everyone is included
3. Compelling vision
4. Clear performance goals
5. One plan
6. Facts and data
7. Propose a plan, "find-a-way" attitude
8. Respect, listen, help, and appreciate each other
9. Emotional resilience ... trust the process
10. Have fun ... enjoy the journey and each other[41]

"Mulally even applauded Mark Fields (who would eventually become his successor) for admitting to a failure in an executive meeting, which at that time, was unheard-of at Ford, and it set the tone for the open and honest communications required for a new culture at the company."[42] Agile managers who function as pioneers inspire others. Schultz, O'Neill, and Mulally inspired their employees in different manners. Schultz reminded employees of the organization's focus around being the third place outside of home and office where people can gather around coffee. O'Neill placed safety at the focus of all that Alcoa did to ensure all employees felt safe. Mulally understand the value of placing people first and helped Ford focus on the customer.

Each manager used a different strategy to inspire their organization. As McKinsey highlighted in a June 2020 report, "empowerment is needed from the very beginning of an agile transformation."[43] Such empowerment is derived from leaders like Schultz, O'Neill, and Mulally

---

[41] "How Alan Mulally saved Ford Motor Company with Four Simple Decisions." March 6, 2018. https://catalystgrowthadvisors.com/2018/03/06/how-alan-mulally-saved-ford-motor-company-with-four-simple-decisions/

[42] Garton, E. 2017. "How to be an Inspiring Leader." *Harvard Business Review,* April 25, 2017. https://hbr.org/2017/04/how-to-be-an-inspiring-leader

[43] Comella-Dorda, S., C. Handscomb, and A. Zaidi. 2020. "Agility to Action: Operationalizing a Value-Driven Agile Blueprint." *McKinsey,* June 16, 2020. https://mckinsey.com/business-functions/organization/our-insights/agility-to-action-operationalizing-a-value-driven-agile-blueprint#

who inspired their employees to be more agile at the individual, team, and organizational level. These three examples, and there are many more, illustrate to any manager operating in a volatile world the need to find out how they can inspire their organization to be more agile. Employees need to feel empowered to change and having an agile leader who functions as a pioneer and inspires others (Principle #18) is an absolute necessity in today's hypercompetitive world as the organization looks to navigate a sustainable path forward.

Questions

Principle #16: Encourage Dialogue

- What percentage of time do you engage in each of the four ways of talking: debate, conversation, dialogue, or discussion?
- Is dialogue a part of your organization's culture?
- Do different departments, units, or offices, engage in more dialogue than others?
- What is the relationship between dialogue and creating a more agile organization?
- When is the last time you encouraged dialogue?
- When is the last time your boss engaged you in a dialogue?
- What is prohibiting you from engaging in dialogue?
- How have you functioned as a pioneer who encourages dialogue recently?

Principle #17: Remain Open-Minded

- How often do you think about the difference between assimilating information compared to accommodating it?
- How open-minded would you consider yourself: not at all, somewhat, very?
- Can you provide at least three examples as to when you were open-minded?
- How would you describe your organization's commitment to being open-minded?

- What is the relationship between being open-minded and creating a more agile organization?
- How uncomfortable do you get when thinking differently?
- Why do you think open-mindedness is such a challenge for most people?
- How often do you invite others to challenge your way of thinking?

Principle #18: Inspire Others

- Who or what has inspired you?
- What role does inspiration play in your organization's culture?
- What is the relationship between agility and inspiration?
- How much time each week do you deliberately think about inspiration as an effective management tool?
- What role do you think inspiration plays in your organization?
- How do you know of you have inspired others?
- Do you consider yourself as someone who inspires others? Why? Why not?
- Have you identified any employees who can contribute to inspiring the organization?

Conclusion

As discussed in the beginning of this publication, today's manager would be unrecognizable to Henri Fayol whose managerial functions involved the verbs planning, organizing, staffing, directing, and controlling. To assist the agile manager in a volatile world, this publication introduced a new way of thinking and shifted managerial functions from verbs to the nouns: curator, architect, conductor, humanist, advocate, and pioneer. This revision from verb to noun reflects the manager's need to shift their thinking from a position of status to one of perspective. Commenting on the need for a different perspective Darrell Rigby noted, "every organization must innovate and agile, done well, frees and facilitates vigorous innovation without sacrificing the efficiency and reliability essential to traditional operations."[1] This shift from verbs to nouns for managerial functions represents a new way of thinking that will allow the manager to develop their agility and understand their position is far more dynamic, empowering, and creative than previously considered. This new way of thinking will change the actual work managers do. And this new way of thinking is available to all managers, regardless of industry, position, title, training, budget, or educational background.

Unfortunately, far too many organizations still reward status quo thinking. Stability, organizational homeostasis, and self-limiting bureaucracy continue to take precedence over agile thinking, risk taking, and transformational change. Antiquated organizational structures, outdated systems of delivery, and entitlement-based cultures are not only reluctant to change, they deliberately resist it. Commenting on the lack of agility among community college leaders across the United States, Jim Riggs observed, "The current way community colleges function, with

---

[1] "Bain & Company Launch a Book to Help Businesses Transform without Chaos." July 1, 2020. https://zawya.com/mena/en/press-releases/story/Bain__Company_launch_a_book_to_help_businesses_transform_without_chaos-ZAWYA20200701093410/

their roots grounded in outdated Weberian management practices, out-moded instructional delivery systems, and archaic approaches to student and institutional support services, simply will not work for institu-tions that are charged with serving as major democratizing forces and economic engines for a changing population, a changing world and a rapidly evolving future."[2] Riggs challenged leaders "to think differently about our colleges, how they operate, and in general, the whole pur-pose for their existence. If community colleges don't start changing soon, they are likely to slide into insignificance."[3] The same could be said for almost every other industry and sector operating around the world today. "Agile managers are not limited by the way it's always been done. In fact, they are suspicious of anything that's been done the same way for too long."[4] While managers continue to build their armamentarium to help create more agile organizations, unexpected external events can serve as an unwelcome catalyst. One such example was the COVID-19 global pandemic of 2020.

While finishing this manuscript the COVID-19 global pandemic continued to wreak havoc on the world's health and economy. As of July 2020, there is no apparent end in sight. Hopes do exist, however, for a vaccine during the next 12 to 18 months. When the pandemic hit the United States during the first quarter of 2020, many organizations shifted most, or all, of their work modality from the physical to the remote within a matter of weeks if not days. Overnight, agility became a necessity. What was once thought of as a theoretical framework to aspire to, became the sole strategy for sustainability. Some organizations adjusted and produced

---

[2] Riggs, J. 2009. "Leadership, Change and the Future of Community Colleges." California State University, The Newsletter for the Doctoral Program in Educational Leadership, Spring 2009. https://csustan.edu/sites/default/files/EdD/documents/EdDirectionsR2LoRes.pdf

[3] Riggs, J. 2009. "Leadership, Change and the Future of Community Colleges." California State University, The Newsletter for the Doctoral Program in Edu-cational Leadership, Spring 2009. https://csustan.edu/sites/default/files/EdD/documents/EdDirectionsR2LoRes.pdf

[4] "15 Key Qualities That Define An Agile Leader." Forbes, June 17, 2020. https://forbes.com/sites/forbescoachescouncil/2020/06/17/15-key-qualities-that-define-an-agile-leader/#55ae18ce7f31

COVID related products, while other entities either temporarily closed or permanently shut their doors since they failed to implement the level of agility required to survive.

According to the World Economic Forum's October 2020 *The Future of Jobs Report* "Automation, in tandem with the COVID-19 recession, is creating a 'double-disruption' scenario for workers." On top of an already stressed global marketplace as a result of the disruptive pandemic-induced lockdowns and economic contraction, technological adoption by companies will transform tasks, jobs and skills by 2025:

- 43 percent of businesses indicate that they are set to reduce their workforce due to technology integration
- 41 percent plan to expand their use of contractors for task-specialized work
- 34 percent plan to expand their workforce due to technology integration

The World Economic Forum estimates that "by 2025, the time spent on current tasks at work by humans and machines will be equal. A significant share of companies also expect to make changes to locations, their value chains, and the size of their workforce due to factors beyond technology in the next five years."[5]

Recognizing the difficulty businesses had in responding to the pandemic, Rebecca Henderson, CEO of Randstad Global Businesses, noted, "The only way to be able to thrive when crisis hits, and subsequently when things stabilize, is to be agile; agile in business strategy, workforce strategy, employee reskilling strategy and tech strategy. That mindset applies both to organizations that faced unprecedented demand during the pandemic as well as companies whose business came to a grinding halt as the economy slowed."[6]

---

[5] World Economic Forum, The Future of Jobs Reports, October 2020. https://www.weforum.org/reports/the-future-of-jobs-report-2020

[6] "Business Agility Critical to Post-Pandemic Workforce, Economic Recovery." June 24, 2020. https://huntscanlon.com/business-agility-critical-to-post-pandemic-workforce-economic-recovery/

It is no surprise then that agility will be a strategic imperative for those organizations around the world figuring out a way to navigate the four phases of economic process related to the global pandemic as identified by Mastercard: containment, stabilization, normalization, and growth.[7] To that end, Josh Bersin emphasized the need for organizations to translate the theoretical framework of agility to a practical one when he wrote "Agile [used to be] a theoretical concept; now, we have to be agile… it's a leadership capability."[8] Much like Henderson and Bersin, Gartner Audit and Risk practice researcher Emily Riley emphasized the necessity of organizations to become more agile and said, "the recent COVID-19 pandemic illustrates the need for an agile response to unexpected risks."[9] With the global pandemic still raging organizations from every industry sector around the world remain engaged in an evolutionary process of recovery known as "The Big Reset" involving four stages: react, respond, return, and transform.[10] Hopefully, *Agility: Management Principles for a Volatile World* can make some small contribution and help managers create the level of agility required for their organization to work through the four stages and succeed in a volatile world.

[7] Clift, K., and A. Court. 2020. "How are Companies Responding to the Coronavirus Crisis? " *World Economic Forum*, March 23, 2020. https://weforum.org/agenda/2020/03/how-are-companies-responding-to-the-coronavirus-crisis-d15bed6137/

[8] Colletta, J. 2020. "How Agility, Empathy are at the Heart of 'The Big Reset." *HR Executive*, June 30, 2020. https://hrexecutive.com/how-agility-empathy-are-at-the-heart-of-the-big-reset/

[9] "Organizations Need an Agile Response to Unexpected Risks." *Help Net Security*, July 1, 2020. https://helpnetsecurity.com/2020/07/01/agile-response-to-unexpected-risks/

[10] Colletta, J. 2020. "How Agility, Empathy are at the Heart of 'The Big Reset'." *HR Executive*, June 30, 2020. https://hrexecutive.com/how-agility-empathy-are-at-the-heart-of-the-big-reset/

Appendixes

Appendix I: The 6 Functions and 18 Principles of an Agile Manager

Function #1: Curator: gathers information, knowledge, and actionable intelligence

- Principle #1: How often do you study the attributes of today's volatile, uncertain, complex, and ambiguous (VUCA) global marketplace?
- Principle #2: How often do you engage in self-reflection on the risks associated with increasing one's agility?
- Principle #3: How often do you ask the relevant questions to help increase the organization's agility?

Function #2: Architect: conceptualizes, builds, and revises the operational blueprint

- Principle #4: How often do you update the organization's mission?
- Principle #5: How often do you design a vision and plan to move forward?
- Principle #6: How often do you cultivate the values of the organization to clarify roles and responsibilities?

Function #3: Conductor: ensures collaboration, skill development, and harmony

- Principle #7: How often do you foster collaboration across departments, functional areas, and offices?

- Principle #8: How often do you demonstrate a commitment to ensuring employees receiving the skill development, training, and education required to succeed?
- Principle #9: How often do you do you nurture relationships with external stakeholders?

Function #4: Humanist: emphasizes the value and agency of human beings

- Principle #10: How often do you establish a humanist culture based on diversity, equity, and inclusion?
- Principle #11: How often do you exhibit an appreciation of the unique qualities of each person?
- Principle #12: How often do you demonstrate compassion, kindness, and empathy?

Function #5: Advocate: communicates the mission, values, and vision

- Principle #13: How often do you create content to help promote the organization?
- Principle #14: How often do you tell stories about the people, clients, and partners?
- Principle #15: How often do you diversify messages across social media platforms and outlets?

Function #6: Pioneer: explores new ideas, products, and services

- Principle #16: How often do you encourage dialogue from employees and others about the organization's products and services?
- Principle #17: How often do you remain opened minded about new ideas?
- Principle #18: How often do you inspire others?

Appendix II: The Agile Manager Self-Assessment

Today's Date: _____

The Agile Manager's Self-Assessment						
	Curator	Architect	Conductor	Humanist	Advocate	Pioneer
Always						
Frequently						
Often						
Sometimes						
Never						

In a given week never means 0 days; sometimes means 1 day; often means 2–3 days, frequently means 4–5 days, and always means 7 days.

Notes:

Appendix III: *Questions*

Principle #1: Understand the Landscape

- How often do you study the macro trends in your industry?
- How do your employees respond when you discuss VUCA trends?
- What are you doing to help them better understand VUCA trends?
- When you do study them how do you relay that information?
- Do you send reports, information, and other items to your team in the hopes they read and understand the need to change?
- How has today's VUCA environment impacted your organization and what changes have you made/do you still need to make, to achieve and sustain growth?
- Do you have a task force devoted to studying the trends and suggesting changes?
- Are you comfortable with having others recommend agile moves?
- Are you practicing the time-honored tradition of micromanagement and telling people what to do and how to do it when it comes to change management?
- How often are you challenging your people to grow and providing them the support to do so?
- How has hyper-connectedness changed your business?
- How comfortable are you with change, especially constant and intense change?
- How well do you manage uncertainty and being able to move forward without knowing?
- How do you respond to complex situations involving multiple factors?
- How often do you thrive in ambiguity?

Principle #2: Identify Risks

- How often do you think about the various types of risks associated with being a manager?
- How often do you identify personal growth risks that could impact being an agile manager?
- What prevents you from thinking differently?
- How often do you catch yourself engaging in conventional thinking?
- What is your decision-making process?
- How often do you look to improve your decision-making process?
- What prevents you from improving your decision-making process?
- Have you noticed the decision-making process of others?
- How often do you travel outside of your comfort zone?
- How comfortable are you being uncomfortable?

Principle #3: Ask Questions

- How often do you think about the critical questions related to the future of your organization?
- How often do you discuss the need to change to remain relevant?
- Does everyone on your team know why they are doing what they are doing? How do you know?
- How often do you walk around and engage in open conversations with employees?
- For those team members working virtually, how often do you check in on them?
- Have you assessed the types of questions you ask employees?
- What attributes do your questions have?
- How have you worked to improve your listening skills lately?
- Now that you have covered the three principles related to the agile manager as a curator, spend time reflecting on your ability to curate information. How has your ability to function as a curator improve?

Principle #4: Update Mission

- How do you know if everyone understands your organization's mission?
- Where is the organization's mission displayed publicly?
- How often do you refer to your mission?
- How often do your employees refer to the mission?
- Does your organization need to update its mission?
- Does the business model of your organization need to be reinvented?
- What skills, traits, or habits can you rely on to help you become more agile as you prepare for an unknown future?
- How comfortable are you becoming irrelevant?
- What are you going to do to help your organization remain relevant?

Principle #5: Design Vision

- How often do you talk about vision?
- When you do talk about vision do you include others in its development?
- How comfortable are you discussing vision publicly?
- How often do you think about corporate social responsibility?
- As an agile manager, what do you think you can do to help promote CSR?
- What skills, traits, or habits can you rely on to design, or redesign, a vision for an organization in a volatile world?
- Which vision story resonates with you the most and why?
- What lessons can you learn from the TOMS story?
- How familiar are you with blue ocean strategies?
- Why do you think organizations find it easy to generate a new idea but difficult to implement it?

Principle #6: Cultivate Values

- What would employees identify as the top five values of your organization?

- What do you think the organization values most?
- How often do you reflect upon your organization's culture?
- What have you done to update your organization's responsibility to its people and surrounding community?
- What values would you like to improve upon in your organization?
- As an agile manager in a volatile world, how can you help cultivate values?
- What has been the impact of external events on your organization's culture?
- How has your organization leveraged its values to navigate difficult times?
- How does your organization's social media presence reflect its values?

Principle #7: Foster Collaboration

- How would you assess the level of collaboration across your organization?
- What is the organization's track record with collaboration across functional units?
- How often do you work to improve cross-departmental collaboration?
- What could you do as an agile manager to foster collaboration?
- What departments could benefit from increased collaboration?
- Are you aware of the concerns regarding internal collaboration? If so, how can you assuage fears, concerns, and issues?
- What skills, traits, or habits can you leverage to foster collaboration?

Principle #8: Commit to Development

- What have you done recently to demonstrate your own professional development?

- How much time does your organization devote to professional development opportunities for employees?
- When is the last time you helped someone grow professionally or personally?
- How often do you spend on your own professional development?
- What can your organization do to help ignite new professional development training opportunities?
- Do you discuss development opportunities during the interview process for new employees?
- What are some internal barriers to providing new professional development opportunities for employees?
- Have you asked employees recently what training opportunities they would like to see the organization offer?

Principle #9: Nurturing Relationships

- Do all members of the organization understand the definition of collaboration?
- Are the organization's goals clear for everyone to understand?
- Are the criteria for selecting collaborative partnerships developed, revised, and finalized by members of the team?
- Has the organization aligned collaborative efforts with its goals?
- Does the organization view collaboration as a critical component of achieving and sustaining growth?
- Are the lines of communication open, clear, and free of judgment?
- When selecting the team members involved for the project, are employees chosen because they have the required skill set for the project or because of their relationship with the manager?
- Are roles clearly defined with the work process of a collaboration project between managers and employees?
- What is the process for identifying, reporting, and resolving issues that arise during the collaboration project?
- How is collaboration measured at the employee level?

Principle #10: Establishing Culture

- How often do you think about culture as a critical force to leverage to create a more agile organization?
- Have you thought about the relationship between agility and culture?
- How would you describe your organization's culture currently?
- Have you surveyed your employee's attitude toward organizational culture?
- What have you done lately to improve the organizational culture?
- Do you clearly understand your role in creating the organizational culture?
- Have you explained to everyone their role in fostering a positive organizational culture?
- What are some barriers, perceived and real, to improving the organizational culture?
- Can everyone clearly articulate your organization's approach to diversity, equity, and inclusion?

Principle #11: Appreciate Uniqueness

- How much time do you spend thinking about the unique traits of each employee?
- Have you assessed your emotional intelligence (EQ)?
- What have you done lately to demonstrate an appreciation of uniqueness among employees?
- Have you asked employees to describe what is important to them in terms of culture?
- What is your view of the organizational culture?
- Have you thought about the relationship between agility and the unique traits of each employee?
- Where do you see areas of improvement in the organizational culture? Is that in alignment with what the employees recorded?

Principle #12: Demonstrate Compassion

- Would you consider the demonstration of compassion a weakness? Why? Why not?
- What is the relationship between your organization's culture and compassion?
- How would you describe your level of compassion toward your employees?
- What have you done lately to demonstrate compassion toward others?
- Have you witnessed employees being compassionate toward one another?
- Where do you think some additional compassion could benefit your organizational culture?
- Do you have difficulty demonstrating compassion? Explain.
- What are some internal barriers to demonstrating additional compassion?

Principle #13: Create Content

- How often do you advocate for your organization, employees, or customers via creating content?
- How can creating content demonstrate agility?
- What skills, traits, or habits could you leverage to create content?
- If you do not create content, why is that?
- If you have created content what has been your experience?
- Do you believe creating content is irrelevant or an unnecessary distraction?
- Have you spent any time reading the content of other leaders who publish their material online or on social media?

Principle #14: Tell Stories

- What stories have had the great impact in your life? Why?
- What is the last story you told about your organization?

- How often do you tell stories about your organization?
- What are three stories you might tell about your organization?
- What channels of communication do you currently use to hear or read about stories?
- Does your organization support storytelling?
- Would telling stories impact the culture?
- What do you think is the relationship between storytelling and agility?
- Do your competitors use stories? If so, how, and what have you learned from studying them?

Principle #15: Diversify Channels

- What social media outlets do you use to advocate for your organization?
- Do you allow employees to post on social media during the day?
- Is what is being shared on the different channels representative of the organizational culture?
- What channels are most used by your employees?
- What are your competitors doing on the different social media channels?
- Does your organization offer any training on helping managers learn about social media?
- How can you improve your role as an advocate on different platforms?

Principle #16: Encourage Dialogue

- What percentage of time do you engage in each of the four ways of talking: debate, conversation, dialogue, or discussion?
- Is dialogue a part of your organization's culture?
- Do different departments, units, or offices, engage in more dialogue than others?
- What is the relationship between dialogue and creating a more agile organization?
- When is the last time you encouraged dialogue?

- When is the last time your boss engaged you in a dialogue?
- What is prohibiting you from engaging in dialogue?
- How have you functioned as a pioneer who encourages dialogue recently?

Principle #17: Remain Open-Minded

- How often do you think about the difference between assimilating information compared to accommodating it?
- How open-minded would you consider yourself: not at all, somewhat, very?
- Can you provide at least three examples as to when you were open-minded?
- How would you describe your organization's commitment to being open-minded?
- What is the relationship between being open-minded and creating a more agile organization?
- How uncomfortable do you get when thinking differently?
- Why do you think open-mindedness is such a challenge for most people?
- How often do you invite others to challenge your way of thinking?

Principle #18: Inspire Others

- Who or what has inspired you?
- What role does inspiration play in your organization's culture?
- What is the relationship between agility and inspiration?
- How much time each week do you deliberately think about inspiration as an effective management tool?
- What role do you think inspiration plays in your organization?
- How do you know of you have inspired others?
- Do you consider yourself as someone who inspires others? Why? Why not?
- Have you identified any employees who can contribute to inspiring the organization?

About the Author

Dr. Michael Edmondson serves as the Dean of Professional Education and Lifelong Learning, the Dean of the College of Professional Studies (Interim) and the Director of NJCU @ Ft. Monmouth (Interim) at New Jersey City University (NJCU).

Prior to joining NJCU, Dr. Edmondson served Augustana College (IL) as an Associate Vice President in the Career/Opportunities/ Research/ Exploration (CORE) Center. Dr. Edmondson and his team created the nation's first undergraduate professional preparation tracking system— The Viking Score.

Awards for his distinguished work include The Heritage Who's Who Among International Business Executives for Lifetime Achievement and the Philadelphia Entrepreneurial Inspiration Award. Dr. Edmondson was selected as a member of the 2013 to 2014 Senior Leadership Academy cosponsored by the Council of Independent Colleges and American Academic Leadership Institute.

Dr. Edmondson has an active speaking, research, and writing agenda with an emphasis on the intersection of personal growth and professional development. He brings a wealth of knowledge regarding organizational culture, career pathways, academic majors, workforce development, the future of work, management principles, leadership strategies, strategic thinking, and the dynamics driving today's volatile, uncertain, complex, and ambiguous global marketplace.

Business Experts Press has published six of Dr. Edmondson's professional development books: *Marketing Your Value: 9 Steps to Navigating Your Career* (2015) *Major in Happiness: Debunking the College Major Fallacies* (2016), *Success: Theory and Practice* (2017), *Strategic Thinking and Writing* (2018), *The Relevance of the Humanities to the 21st Century Workplace* (2019), and *Agility: Management Principles for A Volatile World* (2021).

Dr. Edmondson received a BA in History from Cabrini College, a MA in History from Villanova University, and a PhD in History from Temple University. The Herbert Hoover Presidential Library awarded Dr. Edmondson a research grant that allowed him to complete his dissertation "The Foreign Policy of American Individualism: Herbert Clark Hoover, the Department of Commerce, and Mexico, 1921–1928."

Index

OTHER TITLES IN THE HUMAN RESOURCE MANAGEMENT AND ORGANIZATIONAL BEHAVIOR COLLECTION

- *Strengths Oriented Leadership* by Matt L. Beadle
- *The Successful New CEO* by Christian Muntean
- *Leadership In Disruptive Times* by Sattar Bawany
- *Level-Up Leadership* by Michael J. Provitera
- *The Truth About Collaborating* by Dr. Gail Levitt
- *Uses and Risks of Business Chatbots* by Tania Peitzker
- *Three Key Success Factors for Transforming Your Business* by Michael Hagemann
- *Hiring for Fit* by Janet Webb
- *Successful Recruitment* by Stephen Amos
- *Uniquely Great* by Lucy English
- *The Relevance of Humanities to the 21st Century Workplace* by Michael Edmondson
- *Untenable* by Gary Covert
- *Chief Kickboxing Officer* by Alfonso Asensio
- *Transforming the Next Generation Leaders* by Sattar Bawany

Concise and Applied Business Books

The Collection listed above is one of 30 business subject collections that Business Expert Press has grown to make BEP a premiere publisher of print and digital books. Our concise and applied books are for...

- Professionals and Practitioners
- Faculty who adopt our books for courses
- Librarians who know that BEP's Digital Libraries are a unique way to offer students ebooks to download, not restricted with any digital rights management
- Executive Training Course Leaders
- Business Seminar Organizers

Business Expert Press books are for anyone who needs to dig deeper on business ideas, goals, and solutions to everyday problems. Whether one print book, one ebook, or buying a digital library of 110 ebooks, we remain the affordable and smart way to be business smart. For more information, please visit www.businessexpertpress.com, or contact sales@businessexpertpress.com.